THE BEST-LOVED POEMS OF

James Whitcomb Riley

THE
BEST-LOVED POEMS

OF

James Whitcomb Riley

PUBLISHERS

Grosset & Dunlap

NEW YORK

To

The Children of The Old Times and of These

With changeless love

CONTENTS

WHILE THE HEART BEATS YOUNG

WHILE the heart beats young!—O the
      splendor of the Spring,
With all her dewy jewels on, is not so fair a
      thing!
The fairest, rarest morning of the blossom-time
      of May
Is not so sweet a season as the season of to-day
While Youth's diviner climate folds and holds
      us, close caressed,
As we feel our mothers with us by the touch of
      face and breast;—
Our bare feet in the meadows, and our fancies
      up among
The airy clouds of morning—while the heart
      beats young.

While the heart beats young and our pulses leap
      and dance,
With every day a holiday and life a glad ro-
      mance,—
We hear the birds with wonder, and with won-
      der watch their flight—
Standing still the more enchanted, both of hear-
      ing and of sight,

*When they have vanished wholly,—for, in
  fancy, wing-to-wing*
*We fly to Heaven with them; and, returning,
  still we sing*
*The praises of this lower Heaven with tireless
  voice and tongue,*
*Even as the Master sanctions—while the heart
  beats young.*
*While the heart beats young!—While the heart
  beats young!*
*O green and gold old Earth of ours, with azure
  overhung*
*And looped with rainbows!—grant us yet this
  grassy lap of thine—*
*We would be still thy children, through the
  shower and the shine!*
*So pray we, lisping, whispering, in childish love
  and trust,*
*With our beseeching hands and faces lifted from
  the dust*
*By fervor of the poem, all unwritten and un-
  sung,*
*Thou givest us in answer, while the heart beats
  young.*

THE BEST-LOVED POEMS OF

James Whitcomb Riley

THE RAGGEDY MAN

O THE RAGGEDY MAN! He works fer Pa;
An' he's the goodest man ever you saw!
He comes to our house every day,
An' waters the horses, an' feeds 'em hay;
An' he opens the shed—an' we all ist laugh
When he drives out our little old wobble-ly calf;
An' nen—ef our hired girl says he can—
He milks the cow fer 'Lizabuth Ann.—
   Ain't he a' awful good Raggedy Man?
      Raggedy! Raggedy! Raggedy Man!

W'y, The Raggedy Man—he's ist so good
He splits the kindlin' an' chops the wood;
An' nen he spades in our garden, too,
An' does most things 'at *boys* can't do!—
He clumbed clean up in our big tree
An' shooked a' apple down fer me—
An' nother'n', too, fer 'Lizabuth Ann—
An' nother'n', too, fer The Raggedy Man.—
  Ain't he a' awful kind Raggedy Man?
    Raggedy! Raggedy! Raggedy Man!

An' The Raggedy Man, he knows most rhymes
An' tells 'em, ef I be good, sometimes:
Knows 'bout Giunts, an' Griffuns, an' Elves,
An' the Squidgicum-Squees 'at swallers therselves!
An', wite by the pump in our pasture-lot,
He showed me the hole 'at the Wunks is got,
'At lives 'way deep in the ground, an' can
Turn into me, er 'Lizabuth Ann,
Er Ma er Pa er The Raggedy Man!
  Ain't he a funny old Raggedy Man?
    Raggedy! Raggedy! Raggedy Man!

The Raggedy Man—one time when he
Wuz makin' a little bow-'n'-orry fer me,
Says "When *you're* big like your Pa is,
Air *you* go' to keep a fine store like his—
An' be a rich merchunt—an' wear fine clothes?—
Er what *air* you go' to be, goodness knows!"
An' nen he laughed at 'Lizabuth Ann,
An' I says "'M go' to be a Raggedy Man!—
 I'm ist go' to be a nice Raggedy Man!"
  Raggedy! Raggedy! Raggedy Man!

WHERE SHALL WE LAND

Where shall we land you, sweet?
—SWINBURNE

ALL listlessly we float
     Out seaward in the boat
     That beareth Love.
Our sails of purest snow
Bend to the blue below
   And to the blue above.
     Where shall we land?

We drift upon a tide
Shoreless on every side,
   Save where the eye
Of Fancy sweeps far lands
Shelved slopingly with sands
   Of gold and porphyry.
     Where shall we land?

The fairy isles we see,
Loom up so mistily—
   So vaguely fair,
We do not care to break
Fresh bubbles in our wake
   To bend our course for there.
     Where shall we land?

The warm winds of the deep
Have lulled our sails to sleep,
   And so we glide
Careless of wave or wind,
Or change of any kind,
   Or turn of any tide.
     Where shall we land?

We droop our dreamy eyes
Where our reflection lies
   Steeped in the sea,
And, in an endless fit
Of languor, smile on it
   And its sweet mimicry.
     Where shall we land?

"Where shall we land?" God's grace!
I know not any place
   So fair as this—
Swung here between the blue
Of sea and sky, with you
   To ask me, with a kiss,
     "Where shall we land?"

MAYMIE'S STORY OF RED RIDING-HOOD

W'Y, one time wuz a little-weenty dirl,
     An' she wuz named Red Riding-Hood,
          'cause her—
Her *Ma* she maked a little red cloak fer her
'At turnt up over her head.—An' it 'uz all
Ist one piece o' red cardinul 'at's like
The drate-long stockin's the storekeepers has.—
Oh! it 'uz purtiest cloak in all the world
An' *all* this town er anywheres they is!
An' so, one day, her Ma she put it on
Red Riding-Hood, she did—one day, she did—
An' it 'uz *Sund'y*—'cause the little cloak
It 'uz too nice to wear ist *ever'* day
An' *all* the time!—An' so her Ma, she put
It on Red Riding-Hood—an' telled her not
To dit no dirt on it ner dit it mussed
Ner nothin'! An'—an'—nen her Ma she dot

Her little basket out, 'at Old Kriss bringed
Her wunst—one time, he did. An' nen she fill'
It full o' whole lots an' 'bundance o' dood things t' eat
(Allus my Dran'ma *she* says " 'bundance," too).
An' so her Ma fill' little Red Riding-Hood's
Nice basket all ist full o' dood things t' eat,
An' tell her take 'em to her old Dran'ma—
An' not to *spill* 'em, neever—'cause ef she
'Ud stump her toe an' spill 'em, her Dran'ma
She'll haf to *punish* her!

                    An' nen—An' so
Little Red Riding-Hood she p'omised she
'Ud be all careful nen, an' cross' her heart
'At she won't run an' spill 'em all fer six—
Five—ten—two-hundred-bushel-dollars-gold!
An' nen she kiss' her Ma doo'-by an' went
A-skippin' off—away fur off frough the
Big woods, where her Dran'ma she live at—
    No!—
She didn't do *a-skippin'*, like I said:—
She ist went *walkin'*—careful-like an' slow—
Ist like a little lady—walkin' 'long
As all polite an' nice—an' slow—an' straight—
An' turn her toes—ist like she's marchin' in
The Sund'y-School k-session!

                      An'—an'—so
She 'uz a-doin' along—an' doin' along—

On frough the drate-big woods—'cause her
    Dran'ma
She live 'way, 'way fur off frough the big woods
From *her* Ma's house. So when Red Riding-Hood
Dit to do there, she allus have most fun—
When she do frough the drate-big woods, you
    know.—
'Cause she ain't feard a bit o' anything!
An' so she sees the little hoppty-birds
'At's in the trees, an' flyin' all around,
An' singin' dlad as ef their parunts said
They'll take 'em to the magic-lantern show!
An' she 'ud pull the purty flowers an' things
A-growin' round the stumps.—An' she 'ud ketch
The purty butterflies, an' drasshoppers,
An' stick pins frough 'em—No!—I ist *said* that!—
'Cause she's too dood an' kind an' 'bedient
To *hurt* things thataway.—She'd *ketch* 'em, though,
An' ist *play* wiv 'em ist a little while,
An' nen she'd let 'em fly away, she would,
An' ist skip on ad'in to her Dran'ma's.

An' so, while she 'uz doin' 'long an' 'long,
First thing you know they 'uz a drate-big old
Mean wicked Wolf jumped out 'at wanted t' eat
Her up, but *dassent* to—'cause wite clos't there
They wuz a Man a-choppin' wood, an' you

Could *hear* him.—So the old Wolf he 'uz *feard*
Only to ist be *kind* to her.—So he
Ist 'tended-like he wuz dood friends to her
An' says, "Dood morning, little Red Riding-
    Hood!"—
All ist as kind!
          An' nen Riding-Hood
She say "Dood morning," too—all kind an' nice—
Ist like her Ma she learn'—No!—mustn't say
"Learn'," 'cause *"learn'"* it's unproper.—So she say
It like her *Ma* she *"teached"* her.—An'—so she
Ist says "Dood morning" to the Wolf—'cause she
Don't know ut-tall 'at he's a *wicked* Wolf
An' want to eat her up!
               Nen old Wolf smile
An' say, so kind: "Where air you doin' at?"
Nen little Red Riding-Hood she say: "I'm doin'
To my Dran'ma's, 'cause my Ma say I might."
Nen, when she tell him that, the old Wolf he
Ist turn an' light out frough the big thick woods,
Where she can't see him any more. An' so
She think he's went to *his* house—but he hain't,—
He's went to her Dran'ma's, to be there first—
An' *ketch* her, ef she don't watch mighty sharp
What she's about!

'An' nen when the old Wolf
Dit to her Dran'ma's house, he's purty smart, —
An' so he 'tend-like *he's* Red Riding-Hood,
An' knock at th' door. An' Riding-Hood's Dran'ma
She's sick in bed an' can't come to the door
An' open it. So th' old Wolf knock' *two* times.
An' nen Red Riding-Hood's Dran'ma she says,
"Who's there?" she says. An' old Wolf 'tends-like
    he's
Little Red Riding-Hood, you know, an' make'
His voice soun' ist like hers, an' says: "It's me,
Dran'ma—an' I'm Red Riding-Hood an' I'm
Ist come to *see* you."
        Nen her old Dran'ma
She think it *is* little Red Riding-Hood,
An' so she say: "Well, come in nen an' make
You'se'f at home," she says, " 'cause I'm down sick
In bed, an' got the 'ralgia, so's I can't
Dit up an' let ye in."
           An' so th' old Wolf
Ist march' in nen an' shet the door ad'in,
An' *drowl',* he did, an' *splunge'* up on the bed
An' et up old Miz Riding-Hood 'fore she
Could put her specs on an' see who it wuz.—
An' so she never knowed *who* et her up!

An' nen the wicked Wolf he ist put on
Her nightcap, an' all covered up in bed—
Like he wuz *her,* you know.

                     Nen, purty soon
Here come along little Red Riding-Hood,
An' *she* knock' at the door. An' old Wolf 'tend-
Like *he's* her Dran'ma; an' he say, "Who's there?"
Ist like her Dran'ma say, you know. An' so
Little Red Riding-Hood she say: "It's *me,*
Dran'ma—an' I'm Red Riding-Hood an' I'm
Ist come to *see* you."

                  An' nen old Wolf nen
He cough an' say: "Well, come in nen an' make
You'se'f at home," he says, " 'cause I'm down sick
In bed, an' got the 'ralgia, so's I can't
Dit up an' let ye in."

                 An' so she think
It's her Dran'ma a-talkin'.—So she ist
Open' the door an' come in, an' set down
Her basket, an' taked off her things, an' bringed
A chair an' clumbed up on the bed, wite by
The old big Wolf she thinks is her Dran'ma—
Only she thinks the old Wolf's dot whole lots
More bigger ears, an' lots more whiskers, too,
Than her Dran'ma; an' so Red Riding-Hood
She's kind o' skeered a little. So she says,

"Oh. Dran'ma, what *big eyes* you dot!" An' nen
The old Wolf says: "They're ist big thataway,
'Cause I'm so dlad to see you!"

Nen she says,
"Oh, Dran'ma, what a drate-big nose you dot!"
Nen th' old Wolf says: "It's ist big thataway
Ist 'cause I smell the dood things 'at you bringed
Me in the basket!"

An' nen Riding-Hood
She says, "Oh-me-oh-*my!* Dran'ma! what big
White long sharp teeth you dot!"

Nen old Wolf says:
"Yes—an' they're thataway"—an' drowled—
"They're thataway," he says, "to *eat* you wiv!"
An' nen he ist *jump'* at her.—

But she *scream'*—
An' *scream'*, she did.—So's 'at the Man
'At wuz a-choppin' wood, you know,—*he* hear,
An' come a-runnin' in there wiv his ax;
An', 'fore the old Wolf know' what he's about,
He split his old brains out an' killed him s' quick
It make' his head swim!—An' Red Riding-Hood
She wuzn't hurt at all!

An' the big Man
He tooked her all safe home, he did, an' tell
Her Ma she's all right an' ain't hurt at all

An' old Wolf's dead an' kilied—an' ever'thing!—
So her Ma wuz so tickled an' so proud,
She gived *him* all the dood things t' eat they wuz
'At's in the basket, an' she tell' him 'at
She's much oblige', an' say to "call ad'in."
An' story's honest *truth*—an' all *so,* too!

A SUDDEN SHOWER

BAREFOOTED boys scud up the street,
  Or skurry under sheltering sheds;
And schoolgirl faces, pale and sweet,
  Gleam from the shawls about their heads.

Doors bang; and mother-voices call
  From alien homes; and rusty gates
Are slammed; and high above it all,
  The thunder grim reverberates.

And then, abrupt,—the rain! the rain!—
  The earth lies gasping; and the eyes
Behind the streaming window-pane
  Smile at the trouble of the skies.

The highway smokes; sharp echoes ring;
 The cattle bawl and cowbells clank;
And into town comes galloping
 The farmer's horse, with steaming flank.

The swallow dips beneath the eaves,
 And flirts his plumes and folds his wings;
And under the catawba leaves
 The caterpillar curls and clings.

The bumble-bee is pelted down
 The wet stem of the hollyhock;
And sullenly, in spattered brown,
 The cricket leaps the garden walk.

Within, the baby claps his hands
 And crows with rapture strange and vague;
Without, beneath the rosebush stands
 A dripping rooster on one leg.

THE USED-TO-BE

BEYOND the purple, hazy trees
       Of summer's utmost boundaries;
       Beyond the sands—beyond the seas—
Beyond the range of eyes like these,
   And only in the reach of the
   Enraptured gaze of Memory,
   There lies a land, long lost to me,—
       The land of Used-to-be!

A land enchanted—such as swung
In golden seas when sirens clung
Along their dripping brinks, and sung
To Jason in that mystic tongue
   That dazed men with its melody—
   O such a land, with such a sea
   Kissing its shores eternally,
       Is the fair Used-to-be.

A land where music ever girds
The air with belts of singing-birds,
And sows all sounds with such sweet words,
That even in the low of herds
   A meaning lives so sweet to me,
   Lost laughter ripples limpidly
   From lips brimmed over with the glee
   Of rare old Used-to-be.

Lost laughter, and the whistled tunes
Of boyhood's mouth of crescent runes,
That rounded, through long afternoons,
To serenading plenilunes—
　　When starlight fell so mistily
　　That, peering up from bended knee,
　　I dreamed 'twas bridal drapery
　　　Snowed over Used-to-be.

O land of love and dreamy thoughts,
And shining fields, and shady spots
Of coolest, greenest grassy plots,
Embossed with wild forget-me-nots!—
　　And all ye blooms that longingly
　　Lift your fair faces up to me
　　Out of the past, I kiss in ye
　　　The lips of Used-to-be.

CHRISTINE'S SONG

U P in Tentoleena Land—
        Tentoleena! Tentoleena!
All the Dollies, hand in hand,
        Mina, Nainie, and Serena,
Dance the Fairy fancy dances,
With glad songs and starry glances,
Lisping roundelays; and, after,
Bird-like interludes of laughter
Strewn and scattered o'er the lawn
Their gilt sandals twinkle on
Through light mists of silver sand—
        Up in Tentoleena Land.

Up in Tentoleena Land—
      Tentoleena! Tentoleena!
Blares the eerie Elfin band—
      Trumpet, harp and concertina—
Larkspur bugle—honeysuckle
Cornet, with a quickstep chuckle
In its golden throat; and, maybe,
Lilies-of-the-valley they be
Baby-silver-bells that chime
Musically all the time,
Tossed about from hand to hand—
      Up in Tentoleena Land.

Up in Tentoleena Land—
      Tentoleena! Tentoleena!
Dollies dark, and blonde and bland—
      Sweet as musk-rose or verbena—
Sweet as moon-blown daffodillies,
      Or wave-jostled water-lilies,
Yearning to'rd the rose-mouths, ready
Leaning o'er the river's eddy,—
Dance, and glancing fling to you,
Through these lines you listen to,
Kisses blown from lip and hand
      Out of Tentoleena Land!

BUB SAYS

THE moon in the sky is a custard-pie,
    An' the clouds is the cream pour'd o'er it,
An' all o' the glittering stars in the sky
    Is the powdered sugar for it.

●   ●   ■   ●   ■   ●   ■   ●   ●

Johnts—he's proudest boy in town—
'Cause his Mommy she cut down
His Pa's pants fer Johnts—an' there
Is 'nuff left fer *'nother* pair!

●   ●   ■   ●   ≈   ≈   ●   ●   ●

One time, when her Ma was gone,
Little Elsie she put on
All her Ma's fine clothes—an' black
Grow-grain-silk, an' sealskin-sack;
Nen while she wuz flouncin' out
In the hall an' round about
Some one knocked, an' Elsie she
Clean forgot an' run to see
Who's there at the door—an' saw
Mighty quick at wuz her Ma.
But ef she ain't saw at all,
She'd a-knowed her parasol!

*   *   *   *   *   *   *   *   *

Gran'pas an' Gran'mas is funniest folks!—
Don't be jolly, ner tell no jokes,
Tell o' the weather an' frost an' snow
O' that cold New Year's o' long ago;
And then they sigh at each other an' cough
An' talk about suddently droppin' off.

THE LISPER

ELSIE MINGUS *lisps,* she does!
She lives wite acrosst from us
In Miz. Ayers'uz house 'at she
Rents part to the Mingusuz.—
Yes, an' Elsie plays wiv me.

Elsie lisps so, she can't say
Her own name, ist *anyway!*—
She says *"Elthy"*—like they wuz
Feathers on her words, an' they
Ist stick on her tongue like fuzz.

My! she's *purty,* though!—An' when
She *lisps,* w'y, she's purty *nen!*
When she telled me, wunst, her doll
Wuz so "thweet," an' I p'ten'
I lisp, too,—she laugh'—'at 's all!—

40

She don't never git mad none—
'Cause she know I'm ist in fun.—
  Elsie she ain't one bit sp'iled.—
Of all childerns—ever' one—
  She's the *ladylikest* child!—

My Ma *say* she is! One time
Elsie start to say the rhyme,
  "Thing a thong o' thixpenth"—*Wheel*
I ist *yell!* An' Ma say I'm
  Unpolite as I can be!

Wunst I went wiv Ma to call
On Elsie's Ma, an' eat an' all;
  An' nen Elsie, when we've et,
An' we 're playin' in the hall,
  Elsie say: It's etikett

Fer young gentlemens, like me,
Eatin' when they's *company,*
  Not to never ever crowd
Down their food, ner "thip their tea
  Ner thup thoop so awful loud!"

AT UTTER LOAF

I

AN afternoon as ripe with heat
    As might the golden pippin be
    With mellowness if at my feet
It dropped now from the apple-tree
My hammock swings in lazily.

II

The boughs about me spread a shade
    That shields me from the sun, but weaves
    With breezy shuttles through the leaves
Blue rifts of skies, to gleam and fade
    Upon the eyes that only see
    Just of themselves, all drowsily.

III

Above me drifts the fallen skein
    Of some tired spider, looped and blown,
As fragile as a strand of rain,
    Across the air, and upward thrown
    By breaths of hay-fields newly mown—
So glimmering it is and fine,
I doubt these drowsy eyes of mine.

IV

Far-off and faint as voices pent
   In mines, and heard from underground,
Come murmurs as of discontent,
   And clamorings of sullen sound
The city sends me, as, I guess,
To vex me, though they do but bless
Me in my drowsy fastnesses.

V

I have no care. I only know
   My hammock hides and holds me here
   In lands of shade a prisoner:
While lazily the breezes blow
   Light leaves of sunshine over me,
And back and forth and to and fro
   I swing, enwrapped in some hushed glee,
   Smiling at all things drowsily.

BUD'S FAIRY TALE

SOME peoples thinks they ain't no Fairies *now*
No more yet!—But they *is,* I bet! 'Cause ef
They *wuzn't* Fairies, nen I' like to know
Who'd w'ite 'bout Fairies in the books, an' tell
What Fairies *does,* an' how their *picture* looks,
An' all an' ever'thing! W'y, ef they don't
Be Fairies any more, nen little boys
'Ud ist *sleep* when they go to sleep an' won't
Have ist no dweams at all,—'cause Fairies—*good*
Fairies—they're a-purpose to make dweams!
But they *is* Fairies—an' I *know* they is!
'Cause one time wunst, when it's all Summer-time,
An' don't haf to be no fires in the stove
Er fireplace to keep warm wiv—ner don't haf
To wear old scwatchy flannen shirts at all,
An' ain't no fweeze—ner cold—ner snow!—An'—an'

44

Old skweeky twees got all the gween leaves on
An' ist keeps noddin', noddin' all the time,
Like they 'uz lazy an' a-twyin' to go
To sleep an' couldn't, 'cause the wind won't quit
A-blowin' in 'em, an' the birds won't stop
A-singin', so's they *kin*.—But twees *don't* sleep,
I guess! But *little boys* sleeps—an' *dweams,* too.—
An' that's a sign they's Fairies.

                       So, one time,
When I be'n playin' "Store" wunst over in
The shed of their old stable, an' Ed Howard
He maked me quit a-bein' pardners, 'cause
I dwinked the 'tend-like sody-water up
An' et the shore-'nuff crackers,—w'y, nen I
Clumbed over in our garden where the gwapes
Wuz purt' nigh ripe: An' I wuz ist a-layin'
There on th' old cwooked seat 'at Pa maked in
Our arber,—an' so I 'uz layin' there
A-whittlin' beets wiv my new dog-knife, an'
A-lookin' witc up thue the twimbly leaves—
An' wuzn't 'sleep at all!—An'-sir!—first thing
You know, a little *Fairy* hopped out there!—
A *leetle-teenty Fairy!—hope-may-die!*
An' he look' down at me, he did—an' he
Ain't bigger'n a *yellerbird!*—an' he
Say "Howdy-do!" he did—an' I could *hear,*

Him—ist as *plain!*

    Nen *I* say "Howdy-do!"
An' he say *"I'm* all hunky, Nibsey; how
Is *your* folks comin' on?"

     An' nen I say
"My name ain't *'Nibsey,'* neever—my name's
  Bud.—
An' what's *your* name?" I says to him.

      An' he
Ist laugh an' say, " *'Bud's'* awful *funny* name!"
An' he ist laid back on a big bunch o' gwapes
An' laugh' an' laugh', he did—like somebody
'Uz tick-el-un his feet!

     An' nen I say—
"What's *your* name," nen I say, "afore you bu'st
Yo'se'f a-laughin' 'bout *my* name?" I says.
An' nen he dwy up laughin'—kind o' mad—
An' say, "W'y, *my* name's *Squidjicum,"* he says.
An' nen *I* laugh an' say—*"Gee!* what a name!"
An' when I make fun of his name, like that,
He ist git awful mad an' spunky, an'
'Fore you know, he gwabbed holt of a vine—
A big long vine 'at's danglin' up there, an'
He ist helt on wite tight to that, an' down
He swung quick past my face, he did, an' ist
Kicked at me hard's he could!

      But I'm too quick

Fer *Mr. Squidjicum!* I ist weached out
An' ketched him, in my hand—an' helt him, too,
An' *squeezed* him, ist like little wobins when
They can't fly yet an' git flopped out their nest.
An' nen I turn him all wound over, an'
Look at him clos't, you know—wite clos't,—'cause ef
He *is* a Fairy, w'y, I want to see
The *wings* he's got.—But he's dwessed up so fine
'At I can't *see* no wings.—An' all the time
He's twyin' to kick me yet: An' so I take
F'esh holts an' *squeeze* ag'in—an' harder, too;
An' I says, *"Hold up, Mr. Squidjicum!—*
You're kickin' the w'ong man!" I says; an' nen
I ist *squeeze'* him, purt' nigh my *best,* I did—
An' I heerd somepin' bu'st!—An' nen he cwied
An' says, "You better look out what you're doin'!—
You' bu'st my spider-web suspenners, an'
You' got my wose-leaf coat all cwinkled up
So's I can't go to old Miss Hoodjicum's
Tea-party, 's afternoon!"
       An' nen I says —
"Who's 'old Miss Hoodjicum'?" I says.
          An' he
Says, "Ef you lemme loose I'll tell you."
            So
I helt the little skeezics 'way fur out

In one hand—so's he can't jump down t' th' ground,
Wivout a-gittin' all stove up: an' nen
I says, "You're loose now.—Go ahead an' tell
'Bout the 'tea-party' where you're goin' at
So awful fast!" I says.

                    An' nen he say,—
"No use to *tell* you 'bout it, 'cause you won't
Believe it, 'less you go there your own se'f
An' see it wiv your own two eyes!" he says.
An' *he* says: "Ef you lemme *shore-'nuff* loose,
An' p'omise 'at you'll keep wite still, an' won't
Tetch nothin' 'at you see—an' never tell
Nobody in the world—an' lemme loose—
W'y, nen I'll *take* you there!"

                        But I says, "Yes
An' ef I let you loose, you'll *run!*" I says.
An' he says, "No, I won't!—I hope-may-die!"
Nen I says, "Cwoss your heart you won't!"

                                An' he
Ist cwoss his heart; an' nen I reach an' set
The little feller up on a long vine—
An' he 'uz so tickled to git loose ag'in,
He gwab the vine wiv boff his little hands
An' ist take an' turn in, he did, an' skin
'Bout forty-'leben cats!

                    Nen when he git

Thue whirlin' wound the vine, an' set on top
Of it ag'in, w'y, nen his "wose-leaf coat"
He bwag so much about, it's ist all tored
Up, an' ist hangin' strips an' rags—so he
Look like his Pa's a dwunkard. An' so nen
When he see what he's done—a-actin' up
So smart,—he's awful mad, I guess; an' ist
Pout out his lips an' twis' his little face
Ist ugly as he kin, an' set an' tear
His whole coat off—an' sleeves an' all.—An' nen
He wad it all togevver an' ist *th'ow*
It at me ist as hard as he kin dwive!

An' when I weach to ketch him, an' 'uz goin'
To give him 'nuvver squeezin', *he ist flewed
Clean up on top the arbor!*—'Cause, you know,
They *wuz* wings on him—when he tored his *coat*
Clean off—they *wuz* wings *under there*. But they
Wuz purty wobbly-like an' wouldn't work
Hardly at all—'cause purty soon, when I
Th'owed clods at him, an' sticks, an' got him shooed
Down off o' there, he come a-floppin' down
An' lit k-bang! on our old chicken-coop,
An' ist laid there a-whimper'n' like a child!
An' I tiptoed up wite clos't, an' I says, "What's
The matter wiv ye, Squidjicum?"

Says: "Dog-gone! when my wings gits stwaight
    ag'in,
Where you all *crumpled* 'em," he says, "I bet
I'll ist fly clean away an' won't take you
To old Miss Hoodjicum's at all!" he says.
An' nen I ist weach out wite quick, I did,
An' gwab the sassy little snipe ag'in—
Nen tooked my top-stwing an' tie down his wings
So's he *can't* fly, 'less'n I want him to!
An' nen I says: "Now, Mr. Squidjicum,
You better ist light out," I says, "to old
Miss Hoodjicum's, an' show *me* how to git
There, too," I says; "er ef you don't," I says,
"I'll climb up wiv you on our buggy-shed
An' push you off!" I says.

                        An' nen he say
All wite, he'll show me there; an' tell me nen
To set him down wite easy on his feet,
An' loosen up the stwing a little where
It cut him under th' arms. An' nen he says,
"Come on!" he says; an' went a-limpin' 'long
The garden-paph—an' limpin' 'long an' 'long
Tel—purty soon he come on 'long to where's
A grea'-big cabbage-leaf. An' he stoop down
An' say, "Come on inunder here wiv me!"

So *I* stoop down an' crawl inunder there,
Like he say.

         An' inunder there's a grea'-
Big clod, they is—a' awful grea'-big clod!
An' nen he says, *"Woll this-here clod away!"*
An' so I woll' the clod away. An' nen
It's all wet, where the dew'z inunder where
The old clod wuz.—An' nen the Fairy he
Git on the wet-place: Nen he say to me,
"Git on the wet-place, too!" An' nen he say,
"Now hold yer breff an' shet yer eyes!" he says,
"Tel I say *Squinchy-winchy!"* Nen he say—
Somepin' *in Dutch,* I guess.—An' nen I felt
Like we 'uz sinkin' down—an' sinkin' down!—
Tel purty soon the little Fairy weach
An' pinch my nose an' yell at me an' say,
"Squinchy-winchy! Look wherever you please!"
Nen when I looked—Oh! they 'uz purtiest place
Down there you ever saw in all the World!—
They 'uz ist *flowers* an' *woses*—yes, an' *twees*
Wiv *blossoms* on an' *big wipe apples* boff!
An' butterflies, they wuz—an' hummin'-birds—
An' *yeller*birds an' *blue*birds—yes, an' *wed!—*
An' ever'wheres an' all awound 'uz vines
Wiv wipe p'serve-pears on 'em!—Yes, an' all
An' ever'thing 'at's ever growin' in

A garden—er canned up—all wipe at wunst!—
It wuz ist like a garden—only it
'Uz ist a *little bit* o' garden—'bout big wound
As ist our twun'el-bed is.—An' all wound
An' wound the little garden's a gold fence—
An' little gold gate, too—an' ash-hopper
'At's all gold, too—an' ist full o' gold ashes!
An' wite in th' middle o' the garden wuz
A little gold house, 'at's ist 'bout as big
As ist a bird-cage is: An' *in* the house
They 'uz whole-lots *more* Fairies there—'cause I
Picked up the little house, an' peeked in at
The winders, an' I see 'em all in there
Ist *buggin'* round! An' Mr. Squidjicum
He twy to make me quit, but I gwab *him*
An' poke him down the chimbly, too, I did!—
An' y'ort to see *him* hop out 'mongst 'em there!—
Ist like he 'uz the boss an' ist got back!—
"Hain't ye got on them-air dew-dumplin's yet?"
He says.

     An' they says no.

         An' nen he says—
"Better git at 'em nen!" he says, *"wite quick—*
'Cause old Miss Hoodjicum's a-comin'!"

            Nen
They all set wound a little gold tub—an'

All 'menced a-peelin' dewdwops, ist like they
'Uz *peaches*.—An', it looked so funny, I
Ist laugh' out loud, an' *dwopped* the little house,—
An' 't bu'sted like a soap-bubble!—an' 't skeered
Me so, I—I—I—I,—it skeered me so,—
I—ist *waked* up.—No! I *ain't* be'n *asleep*
An' *dweam* it all, like *you* think,—but it's shore
Fer-certain *fact* an' cwoss my heart it is!

THE MAN IN THE MOON

SAID The Raggedy Man, on a hot afternoon:
    My!
        Sakes!
            What a lot o' mistakes
Some little folks makes on The Man in the Moon!
But people that's be'n up to *see* him, like *me,*
And calls on him frequent and intimuttly,
Might drop a few facts that would interest you
    Clean!
        Through!—
           If you wanted 'em to—
    Some *actual* facts that might interest you!

O The Man in the Moon has a crick in his back;
    Whee!
        Whimm!
            Ain't you sorry for him?
And a mole on his nose that is purple and black;
And his eyes are so weak that they water and run
If he dares to *dream* even he looks at the sun,—
So he jes dreams of stars, as the doctors advise—
    My!
        Eyes!
            But isn't he wise—
To jes dream of stars, as the doctors advise?

And The Man in the Moon has a boil on his ear—
    Whee!
        Whing!
            What a singular thing!
I know! but these facts are authentic, my dear,—
There's a boil on his ear; and a corn on his chin—
He calls it a dimple—but dimples stick in—
Yet it might be a dimple turned over, you know!
    Whang!
        Ho!
            Why, certainly so!—
It might be a dimple turned over, you know!

And The Man in the Moon has a rheumatic knee—
 Gee!
  Whizz!
   What a pity that is!
And his toes have worked round where his heels
 ought to be.—
So whenever he wants to go North he goes *South,*
And comes back with porridge-crumbs all round his
 mouth,
And he brushes them off with a Japanese fan,
 Whing!
  Whann!
   What a marvelous man!
What a very remarkably marvelous man!

'N' The Man in the Moon, sighed The Raggedy Man,
 Gits!
  So!
   Sullonesome, you know,—
Up there by hisse'f sence creation began!—
That when *I* call on him and then come away,
He grabs me and holds me and begs me to stay,—
Till—*Well!* if it wasn't fer *Jimmy-cum-jim,*
 Dadd!
  Limb!
   I'd go pardners with him—
Jes jump my job here and be pardners with *him!*

KISSING THE ROD

O HEART of mine, we shouldn't
  Worry so!
 What we've missed of calm we couldn't
  Have, you know!
What we've met of stormy pain,
And of sorrow's driving rain,
We can better meet again,
  If it blow!

We have erred in that dark hour
  We have known,
When our tears fell with the shower,
  All alone!—
Were not shine and shower blent
As the gracious Master meant?—
Let us temper our content
  With His own.

For, we know, not every morrow
  Can be sad;
So, forgetting all the sorrow
  We have had,
Let us fold away our fears,
And put by our foolish tears,
And through all the coming years
  Just be glad.

LET SOMETHING GOOD BE SAID

WHEN over the fair fame of friend or foe
    The shadow of disgrace shall fall, instead
Of words of blame, or proof of thus and so,
    Let something good be said.

Forget not that no fellow-being yet
    May fall so low but love may lift his head:
Even the cheek of shame with tears is wet,
    If something good be said.

No generous heart may vainly turn aside
    In ways of sympathy; no soul so dead
But may awaken strong and glorified,
    If something good be said.

And so I charge ye, by the thorny crown,
    And by the cross on which the Saviour bled,
And by your own soul's hope of fair renown,
    Let something good be said!

THE FUNNIEST THING IN THE WORLD

THE funniest thing in the world, I know,
    Is watchin' the monkeys 'at's in the show!—
    Jumpin' an' runnin' an' racin' roun',
'Way up the top o' the pole; nen down!
First they're here, an' nen they're there,
An' ist a'most any an' ever'where!—
Screechin' an' scratchin' wherever they go,
They're the funniest thing in the world, I know!

They're the funniest thing in the world, I think:—
Funny to watch 'em eat an' drink;
Funny to watch 'em a-watchin' us,
An' actin' 'most like grown folks does!—
Funny to watch 'em p'tend to be
Skeerd at their tail 'at they happen to see;—
But the funniest thing in the world they do
Is never to laugh. like me an' you!

SOME SCATTERING REMARKS OF BUB'S

WUNST I tooked our pepper-box lid
An' cut little pie-dough biscuits, I did,
An' cooked 'em on our stove one day
When our hired girl she said I may.

Honey's the *goodest* thing—Oo-*ooh!*
An' blackburry-pies is goodest, too!
But wite hot biscuits, ist soakin' wet
Wiv tree-mullasus, is goodest yet!

Miss Maimie she's my Ma's friend,—an'
She's purtiest girl in all the lan'!—
An' sweetest smile an' voice an' face—
An' eyes ist looks like p'serves tas'e!

I *ruther* go to the Circus-show;
But, 'cause my *parunts* told me so,
I ruther go to the Sund'y School,
'Cause there I learn the goldun rule.

Say, Pa,—what *is* the goldun rule
'At's allus at the Sund'y School?

THE CIRCUS-DAY PARADE

OH, THE Circus-Day Parade! How the bugles
played and played!
And how the glossy horses tossed their flossy manes
and neighed,
As the rattle and the rhyme of the tenor-drummer's time
Filled all the hungry hearts of us with melody sublime!

How the grand band-wagon shone with a splender all
its own,
And glittered with a glory that our dreams had never
known!
And how the boys behind, high and low of every kind,
Marched in unconscious capture, with a rapture
undefined!

How the horsemen, two and two, with their plumes of
    white and blue,
And crimson, gold and purple, nodding by at me and
    you,
Waved the banners that they bore, as the Knights in days
    of yore,
Till our glad eyes gleamed and glistened like the spangles
    that they wore!

How the graceless-graceful stride of the elephant was
    eyed,
And the capers of the little horse that cantered at his side!
How the shambling camels, tame to the plaudits of their
    fame,
With listless eyes came silent, masticating as they came.

How the cages jolted past, with each wagon battened fast,
And the mystery within it only hinted of at last
From the little grated square in the rear, and nosing there
The snout of some strange animal that sniffed the outer
    air!

And, last of all, The Clown, making mirth for all the
    town,
With his lips curved ever upward and his eyebrows ever
    down,

And his chief attention paid to the little mule that played
A tattoo on the dashboard with his heels, in the Parade.

Oh! the Circus-Day Parade! How the bugles played and
        played!
And how the glossy horses tossed their flossy manes and
        neighed,
As the rattle and the rhyme of the tenor-drummer's time
Filled all the hungry hearts of us with melody sublime!

ALMOST BEYOND ENDURANCE

I AIN'T a-goin' to cry no more no more!
    I'm got ear-ache, an' Ma can't make
      It quit a-tall;
      An' Carlo bite my rubber-ball
  An' puncture it; an' Sis she take
An' poke' my knife down through the stable-floor
    An' loozed it—blame it all!
But I ain't goin' to cry no more no more!

An' Aunt Mame *wrote* she's comin', an' she *can't*—
    Folks is come *there!*—An' I don't care
      She *is* my Aunt!
      An' my eyes stings; an' I'm
    Ist coughin' all the time,
An' hurts me so, an' where my side's so sore
    Grampa felt where, an' he
    Says "Mayby it's *pleurasy!*"
But I ain't goin' to cry no more no more!

An' I clumbed up an' nen falled off the fence,
  An' Herbert he ist laugh at me!
    An' my fi'-cents
It sticked in my tin bank, an' I ist tore
  Purt'-nigh my thumbnail off, a-tryin' to git
  It out—nen *smash* it!—An' it's in there yit!
But I ain't goin' to cry no more no more!

Oo! I'm so wickud!—An' my breath's so *hot*—
  Ist like I run an' don't res' none
But ist run on when I ought to not;
    Yes, an' my chin
  An' lips 's all warpy, an' teeth's so fast,
  An' 's a place in my throat I can't swaller past—
    An' they all hurt so!—
    An' oh, my-oh!
  I'm a-startin' ag'in—
I'm a-*startin'* ag'in, but I *won't,* fer shore!—
I ist ain't goin' to cry no more no more!

LOCKERBIE STREET

SUCH a dear little street it is, nestled away
  From the noise of the city and heat of the day,
  In cool shady coverts of whispering trees,
With their leaves lifted up to shake hands with the
    breeze
Which in all its wide wanderings never may meet
With a resting-place fairer than Lockerbie Street!

There is such a relief, from the clangor and din
Of the heart of the town, to go loitering in
Through the dim, narrow walks, with the sheltering
    shade
Of the trees waving over the long promenade,
And littering lightly the ways of our feet
With the gold of the sunshine of Lockerbie Street.

And the nights that come down the dark pathways of
    dusk,
With the stars in their tresses, and odors of musk
In their moon-woven raiments, bespangled with dews,
And looped up with lilies for lovers to use
In the songs that they sing to the tinkle and beat
Of their sweet serenadings through Lockerbie Street.

O my Lockerbie Street! You are fair to be seen—
Be it noon of the day, or the rare and serene
Afternoon of the night—you are one to my heart,
And I love you above all the phrases of art,
For no language could frame and no lips could repeat
My rhyme-haunted raptures of Lockerbie Street.

HER LONESOMENESS

WHEN little Elizabeth whispers
    Her morning-love to me,
    Each word of the little lisper's,
As she clambers on my knee—
Hugs me and whispers, "Mommy,
  Oh, I'm so glad it's day
  And the night's all gone away!"
How it does thrill and awe me,—
  "The night's all gone away!"

"Sometimes I wake, all listenin',"
  She sighs, "and all's so still!—
The moon and the stars half-glistenin'
  Over the window-sill;—
And I look where the gas's pale light
  Is all turned down in the hall—
  And you ain't here at all!—
And oh, how I wish it was daylight!
  —And you ain't here at all!

"And oh," she goes eerily whining
   And laughing, too, as she speaks,
"If only the sun kept shining
   For weeks and weeks and weeks!—
For the world's so dark, without you,
   And the moon's turned down so low—
   'Way in the night, you know,—
And I get so lonesome about you!—
   'Way in the night, you know!"

THE RAGGEDY MAN ON CHILDREN

CHILDERN—take 'em as they run—
You kin *bet* on, ev'ry one!—
Treat 'em right and reco'nize
Human souls is all one size.

Jevver think?—the world's best men
Wears the same souls they had when
They run barefoot—'way back where
All these little childern air.

Heerd a boy, not long ago,
Say his parents *sassed* him so,
He'd *correct* 'em ef he could,—
Then be good ef *they'd* be good.

THE HIRED MAN'S FAITH IN CHILDREN

I BELIEVE *all* childern's good,
Ef they're only *understood*,—
Even *bad* ones 'pears to me
'S jes' as good as they kin be!

THE NINE LITTLE GOBLINS

THEY all climbed up on a high board-fence—
 Nine little goblins, with green-glass eyes—
Nine little goblins that had no sense,
And couldn't tell coppers from cold mince-pies;
 And they all climbed up on the fence, and sat—
 And I asked them what they were staring at.

And the first one said, as he scratched his head
 With a queer little arm that reached out of his ear,
And rasped its claws in his hair so red—
 "This is what this little arm is fer!"
 And he scratched and stared, and the next one said,
 "How on earth do *you* scratch your head?"

And he laughed like the screech of a rusty hinge—
    Laughed and laughed till his face grew black;
And when he choked, with a final twinge
    Of his stifling laughter, he thumped his back
        With a fist that grew on the end of his tail
        Till the breath came back to his lips so pale.

And the third little goblin leered round at me—
    And there were no lids on his eyes at all—
And he clucked one eye, and he says, says he,
    "What is the style of your socks this fall?"
        And he clapped his heels—and I sighed to see
        That he had hands where his feet should be.

Then a bald-faced goblin, gray and grim,
    Bowed his head, and I saw him slip
His eyebrows off, as I looked at him,
    And paste them over his upper lip;
        And then he moaned in remorseful pain—
        "Would—ah, would I'd me brows again!"

And then the whole of the goblin band
    Rocked on the fence-top to and fro,
And clung, in a long row, hand in hand,
    Singing the songs that they used to know—
        Singing the songs that their grandsires sung
        In the goo-goo days of the goblin-tongue.

And ever they kept their green-glass eyes
 Fixed on me with a stony stare—
Till my own grew glazed with a dread surmise,
 And my hat whooped up on my lifted hair,
  And I felt the heart in my breast snap to,
  As you've heard the lid of a snuff-box do.

And they sang: "You're asleep! There is no board
  fence,
 And never a goblin with green-glass eyes!—
'Tis only a vision the mind invents
 After a supper of cold mince-pies,—
  And you're doomed to dream this way," they
  said,—
   "And you shan't wake up till you're clean plum
   dead!"

THE PIXY PEOPLE

IT was just a very
    Merry fairy dream!—
All the woods were airy
    With the gloom and gleam;
Crickets in the clover
    Clattered clear and strong,
And the bees droned over
    Their old honey-song.

In the mossy passes,
    Saucy grasshoppers
Leapt about the grasses
    And the thistle-burs;
And the whispered chuckle
    Of the katydid
Shook the honeysuckle
    Blossoms where he hid.

Through the breezy mazes
  Of the lazy June,
Drowsy with the hazes
  Of the dreamy noon,
Little Pixy people
  Winged above the walk,
Pouring from the steeple
  Of a mullein-stalk.

One—a gallant fellow—
  Evidently King,—
Wore a plume of yellow
  In a jewelled ring
On a pansy bonnet,
  Gold and white and blue,
With the dew still on it,
  And the fragrance, too.

One—a dainty lady—
  Evidently Queen,—
Wore a gown of shady
  Moonshine and green,
With a lace of gleaming
  Starlight that sent
All the dewdrops dreaming
  Everywhere she went.

One wore a waistcoat
  Of roseleaves, out and in,
And one wore a faced-coat
  Of tiger-lily-skin;
And one wore a neat coat
  Of palest galingale;
And one a tiny street-coat,
  And one a swallow-tail.

And Ho! sang the King of them
  And Hey! sang the Queen;
And round and round the ring of them
  Went dancing o'er the green;
And Hey! sang the Queen of them,
  And Ho! sang the King—
And all that I had seen of them
  —Wasn't anything!

It was just a very
  Merry fairy dream!—
All the woods were airy
  With the gloom and gleam;
Crickets in the clover
  Clattered clear and strong,
And the bees droned over
  Their old honey-song!

THE PRAYER PERFECT

DEAR Lord! kind Lord!
     Gracious Lord! I pray
   Thou wilt look on all I love,
     Tenderly to-day!
Weed their hearts of weariness;
     Scatter every care
Down a wake of angel-wings
     Winnowing the air.

Bring unto the sorrowing
     All release from pain;
Let the lips of laughter
     Overflow again;
And with all the needy
     O divide, I pray,
This vast treasure of content
     That is mine to-day!

REACH YOUR HAND TO ME

REACH your hand to me, my friend,
  With its heartiest caress—
  Sometime there will come an end
To its present faithfulness—
  Sometime I may ask in vain
  For the touch of it again,
  When between us land or sea
  Holds it ever back from me.

Sometime I may need it so,
  Groping somewhere in the night,
It will seem to me as though
  Just a touch, however light,
    Would make all the darkness day,
    And along some sunny way
    Lead me through an April-shower
    Of my tears to this fair hour.

O the present is too sweet
  To go on forever thus!
Round the corner of the street
  Who can say what waits for us?—
    Meeting—greeting, night and day,
    Faring each the selfsame way—
    Still somewhere the path must end—
    Reach your hand to me, my friend!

MAX AND JIM

MAX an' Jim,
　　They're each other's
Fat an' slim
　　Little brothers.

Max is thin,
　　An' Jim, the fac's is,
Fat ag'in
　　As little Max is!

Their Pa 'lowed
　　He don't know whuther
He's most proud
　　Of one er th'other!

Their Ma says
　　They're both so sweet—*'m!*—
That she guess
　　She'll haf to *eat* 'em!

THE SCHOOLBOY'S FAVORITE

*O*VER *the river and through the wood*
Now Grandmother's cap I spy:
Hurrah for the fun!—Is the pudding done?
Hurrah for the pumpkin pie!
—SCHOOL READER.

Fer any boy 'at's little as me,
  Er any little girl,
That-un's the goodest poetry piece
  In any book in the worl'!
An' ef grown-peoples wuz little ag'in
  I bet they'd say so, too,
Ef *they'd* go see *their* old Gran'ma,
  Like our Pa lets *us* do!

Over the river an' through the wood
Now Gran'mother's cap I spy:
Hurrah fer the fun!—Is the puddin' done?—
Hurrah fer the punkin-pie!

An' 'll tell *you* why 'at's the goodest piece:—
'Cause it's ist like *we* go
To *our* Gran'ma's, a-visitun there,
When our Pa he says so;
An' Ma she fixes my little cape-coat
An' little fuzz-cap; an' Pa
He tucks me away—an' yells "Hoo-ray!"—
An' whacks Old Gray, an' drives the sleigh
Fastest you ever saw!

Over the river an' through the wood
Now Gran'mother's cap I spy:
Hurrah fer the fun!—Is the puddin' done?—
Hurrah fer the punkin-pie!

An' Pa ist snuggles me 'tween his knees—
An' I he'p hold the lines,
An' peek out over the buffalo-robe;—
An' the wind ist *blows!*—an' the snow ist *snows!*
An' the sun ist shines! an' shines! —
An' th' ole horse tosses his head an' coughs
The frost back in our face,—
An' I'd ruther go to my Gran'ma's
Than any other place!

Over the river an' through the wood
  Now Gran'mother's cap I spy:
Hurrah fer the fun!—Is the puddin' done?—
  Hurrah fer the punkin-pie!

An' all the peoples they is in town
  Watches us whizzin' past
To go a-visitun our Gran'ma's,
  Like we all went there last;—
But *they* can't go, like ist *our* folks
  An' Johnny an' Lotty, and three
Er four neighber childerns, an' Rober-ut Volney,
  An' Charley an' Maggy an' me!

Over the river an' through the wood
  Now Gran'mother's cap I spy:
Hurrah fer the fun!—Is the puddin' done?—
  Hurrah fer the punkin-pie!

THE OLD TRAMP

A' OLD Tramp slep' in our stable wunst,
    An' The Raggedy Man he caught
    An' roust him up, an' chased him off
Clean out through our back lot!

An' th' old Tramp hollered back an' said,—
    "You're a *purty* man!—*You* air!—
With a pair o' eyes like two fried eggs,
    An' a nose like a Bartlutt pear!"

AN IMPETUOUS RESOLVE

WHEN little Dickie Swope's a man,
  He's go' to be a Sailor;
  'An' little Hamey Tincher, he's
A-go' to be a Tailor:
Bud Mitchell, he's a-go' to be
  A stylish Carriage-Maker;
An' when *I* grow a grea'-big man,
  I'm go' to be a Baker!

An' Dick'll buy his sailor-suit
  O' Hame; an' Hame'll take it
An' buy as fine a double-rig
  As ever Bud kin make it:
An' nen all three'll drive roun' fer me,
  An' we'll drive off togevver,
A-slingin' pie-crust 'long the road
  Ferever an' ferever!

85

GRANNY

GRANNY'S come to our house,
  And ho! my lawzy-daisy!
    All the childern round the place
  Is ist a-runnin' crazy!
Fetched a cake fer little Jake,
  And fetched a pie fer Nanny,
And fetched a pear fer all the pack
  That runs to kiss their Granny!

Lucy Ellen's in her lap,
  And Wade and Silas-Walker
Both's a-ridin' on her foot,
  And Pollos on the rocker;
And Marthy's twins, from Aunt Marinn's,
  And little Orphant Annie,
All's a-eatin' gingerbread
  And giggle-un at Granny!

Tells us all the fairy tales
    Ever thought er wundered—
And 'bundance o' other stories—
    Bet she knows a hunderd!—
Bob's the one fer "Whittington,"
    And "Golden Locks" fer Fanny!
Hear 'em laugh and clap their hands,
    Listenun' at Granny!

"Jack the Giant-Killer" 's good;
    And "Bean-Stalk" 's another!—
So's the one of "Cinderell' "
    And her old godmother;—
That-un's best of all the rest—
    Bestest one of any,—
Where the mices scampers home,
    Like we runs to Granny!

Granny's come to our house,
    Ho! my lawzy-daisy!
All the childern round the place
    Is ist a-runnin' crazy!
Fetched a cake fer little Jake,
    And fetched a pie fer Nanny,
And fetched a pear fer all the pack
    That runs to kiss their Granny!

THE ORCHARD LANDS OF LONG AGO

THE orchard lands of Long Ago!
O drowsy winds, awake, and blow
The snowy blossoms back to me,
And all the buds that used to be!
Blow back along the grassy ways
Of truant feet, and lift the haze
Of happy summer from the trees
That trail their tresses in the seas
Of grain that float and overflow
The orchard lands of Long Ago!

Blow back the melody that slips
In lazy laughter from the lips
That marvel much if any kiss
Is sweeter than the apple's is.
Blow back the twitter of the birds—
The lisp, the titter, and the words
Of merriment that found the shine
Of summer-time a glorious wine
That drenched the leaves that loved it so,
In orchard lands of Long Ago!

O memory! alight and sing
Where rosy-bellied pippins cling,
And golden russets glint and gleam,
As, in the old Arabian dream,
The fruits of that enchanted tree
The glad Aladdin robbed for me!
And, drowsy winds, awake and fan
My blood as when it overran
A heart ripe as the apples grow
In orchard lands of Long Ago!

A BEAR FAMILY

WUNZT, 'way West in Illinoise,
Wuz two Bears an' their two boys:
An' the two boys' names, you know,
Wuz—like *ours* is,—Jim an' Jo;
An' their parunts' names wuz same's
All big grown-up people's names,—
Ist *Miz* Bear, the neighbers call
'Em, an' *Mister* Bear—'at's all.
Yes—an' Miz Bear scold him, too,
Ist like grown folks *shouldn't* do!
Wuz a grea'-big river there,
An', 'crosst that, 's a mountain where
Old Bear said some day he'd go,
Ef she don't quit scoldin' so!
So, one day when he been down
The river, fishin', 'most to town,

An' come back 'thout no fish a-tall,
An' Jim and Jo they run an' bawl
An' tell their ma their pa hain't fetch'
No fish,—she scold again an' ketch
Her old broom up an' biff him, too.—
An' he ist cry, an' say, "Boo-hoo!
I *told* you what I'd do some day!"
An' he ist turned an' runned away
To where's the grea'-big river there,
An' ist *splunged* in an' swum to where
The mountain's at, 'way th' other side,
An' clumbed up there. An' Miz Bear *cried*—
An' little Jo an' little Jim—
Ist like their ma—bofe cried fer him!—
But he clumbed on, *clean out o' sight,*
He wuz so mad!—An' served 'em right!
Nen—when the Bear got 'way on top
The mountain, he heerd somepin' flop
Its wings—an' somepin' else he heerd
A-rattlin'-like.—An' he wuz *skeered,*
An' looked 'way up, an'—*Mercy sake!*
It wuz a' Eagul an' a *snake!*
An'-sir, the Snake, he bite an' kill'
The Eagul, an' they bofe fall till
They strike the ground—*k'spang-k'spat!*
Wite where the Bear wuz standin' at!
An' when here come the Snake at *him,*

The Bear he think o' little Jim
An' Jo, he did—an' their ma, too,—
All safe at home,—an' he ist flew
Back down the mountain—an' could hear
The old Snake rattlin', sharp an' clear,
Wite clos't behind!—An' Bear he's so
All tired out, by time, you know,
He git down to the river there,
He know' he can't *swim* back to where
His folks is at. But ist wite nen
He see a boat an' six big men
'At's been a-shootin' ducks: An' so
He skeered them out the boat, you know,
An' ist jumped in—an' Snake *he* tried
To jump in, too, but falled outside
Where all the water wuz; an' so
The Bear grabs one the things you row
The boat wiv an' ist whacks the head
Of the old Snake an' kills him dead!—
An' when he's killed him dead, w'y, nen
The old Snake's drownded dead again!
Nen Bear set in the boat an' bowed
His back an' rowed—an' rowed—an' rowed—
Till he's safe home—so tired he can't
Do nothin' but lay there an' pant
An' tell his childern, "Bresh my coat!"

An' tell his wife, "Go chain my boat!"
An' they're so glad he's back, they say
"They *knowed* he's comin' thataway
To ist su'prise the dear ones there!"
An' Jim an' Jo they dried his hair
An' pulled the burs out; an' their ma
She ist set there an' helt his paw
Till he wuz sound asleep, an' nen
She telled him she won't scold again—
     Never—never—never—
     Ferever an' ferever!

THE BUMBLEBEE

YOU better not fool with a Bumblebee!—
Ef you don't think they can sting—you'll see!
They're lazy to look at, an' kindo' go
Buzzin' an' bummin' aroun' so slow,
An' ac' so slouchy an' all fagged out,
Danglin' their legs as they drone about
The hollyhawks 'at they can't climb in
'Ithout ist a-tumble-un out ag'in!
Wunst I watched one climb clean 'way
In a jimpson-blossom, I did, one day,—
An' I ist *grabbed* it—an' nen let go—
An' *"Ooh-ooh! Honey! I told ye so!"*
Says the Raggedy Man; an' he ist run
An' pullt out the stinger, an' don't laugh none,
An' says: "They *has* be'n folks, I guess,
'At thought I wuz predjudust more er less,—
Yit I still muntain 'at a Bumblebee
Wears out his welcome too quick fer me!"

THE TOY PENNY-DOG

MA put my Penny-Dog
　　　Safe on the shelf,
　　　An' left no one home but him,
　Me an' myself;
So I clumbed a big chair
　I pushed to the wall—
But the Toy Penny-Dog
　Ain't there at all!
I went back to Dolly—
　An' *she* 'uz gone too,
An' little Switch 'uz layin' there;—
　An' Ma says *"Boo!"*—
An' there she wuz a-peepin'
　Through the front-room door:
An' I ain't goin' to be bad
　Little girl no more!

OUR BETSY

US childern 's all so lonesome
    We hardly want to *play*
Or skip or swing or anything,—
    'Cause Betsy she's away!
She's gone to see her people
    At her old home.—But then—
Oh! ev'ry child 'll jist be wild
    When she's back here again!

Then it's whoopty-doopty dooden!—
    Whoopty-dooden then!
Oh! it's whoopty-doopty dooden,
    When Betsy's back again!

She's like a mother to us,
    And like a sister, too—
Oh! she's as sweet as things to eat
    When all the dinner 's through!
And hey! to hear her laughin'!
    And ho! to hear her sing!—
To have her back is all we lack
    Of havin' *ev'rything!*

Then it's whoopty-doopty dooden?—
  Whoopty-dooden then!
Oh! it's whoopty-doopty dooden,
  When Betsy's back again!

Oh! some may sail the northern lakes,
  And some to foreign lands,
And some may seek old Nameless Creek,
  Or India's golden sands;
Or some may go to Kokomo,
  And some to Mackinac,—
But I'll go down to Morgantown
  To fetch our Betsy back.

Then it's whoopty-doopty dooden?—
  Whoopty-dooden then!
Oh! it's whoopty-doopty dooden,
  When Betsy's back again!

LULLABY

THE maple strews the embers of its leaves
    O'er the laggard swallows nestled 'neath the
      eaves
And the moody cricket falters in his cry—
    Baby-bye!—
And the lid of night is falling o'er the sky—
    Baby-bye!—
The lid of night is falling o'er the sky!

The rose is lying pallid, and the cup
Of the frosted calla-lily folded up;
And the breezes through the garden sob and sigh—
    Baby-bye!—
O'er the sleeping blooms of summer where they lie—
    Baby-bye!—
O'er the sleeping blooms of summer where they lie!

Yet, Baby—O my Baby, for your sake
This heart of mine is ever wide awake,
And my love may never droop a drowsy eye—
    Baby-bye!—
Till your own are wet above me when I die—
    Baby-bye!—
Till your own are wet above me when I die.

THE DAYS GONE BY

O THE days gone by! O the days gone by!
   The apples in the orchard, and the pathway
      through the rye;
The chirrup of the robin, and the whistle of the quail
As he piped across the meadows sweet as any night-
      ingale;
When the bloom was on the clover, and the blue was in
      the sky,
And my happy heart brimmed over, in the days gone by.

In the days gone by, when my naked feet were tripped
By the honeysuckle tangles where the water-lilies
      dipped,
And the ripples of the river lipped the moss along the
      brink
Where the placid-eyed and lazy-footed cattle came to
      drink,
And the tilting snipe stood fearless of the truant's way-
      ward cry
And the splashing of the swimmer, in the days gone by.

O the days gone by! O the days gone by!
The music of the laughing lip, the luster of the eye;
The childish faith in fairies, and Aladdin's magic ring—
The simple, soul-reposing, glad belief in every thing,—
When life was like a story holding neither sob nor sigh,
In the golden olden glory of the days gone by.

LITTLE COUSIN JASPER

LITTLE Cousin Jasper, he
Don't live in this town, like me,—
He lives 'way to Rensselaer,
An' ist comes to visit here.

He says 'at our court-house square
Ain't nigh big as theirn is there!—
He says their town's big as four
Er five towns like this, an' more!

He says ef his folks moved here
He'd cry to leave Rensselaer—
'Cause they's prairie there, an' lakes,
An' wile-ducks an' rattlesnakes!

Yes, 'n' little Jasper's Pa
Shoots most things you ever saw!—
Wunst he shot a deer, one day,
'At swummed off an' got away.

Little Cousin Jasper went
An' camped out wunst in a tent
Wiv his Pa, an' helt his gun
While he kilt a turrapun.

An' when his Ma heerd o' that,
An' more things his Pa's bin at,
She says, "Yes, 'n' he'll git shot
'Fore he's man-grown, like as not!"

An' they's mussrats there, an' minks,
An' di-dippers, an' chee-winks,—
Yes, 'n' cal'mus-root you chew
All up an' 't 'on't pizen you!

An', in town, 's a flag-pole there—
Highest one 'at's anywhere
In this world!—wite in the street
Where the big mass-meetin's meet.

Yes, 'n' Jasper he says they
Got a brass band there, an' play
On it, an' march up an' down
An' all over round the town!

Wisht our town ain't like it is!—
Wisht it's ist as big as his!
Wisht 'at *his* folks they'd move *here*,
An' *we'd* move to Rensselaer;

IRY AND BILLY AND JO

A TINTYPE

IRY an' Billy an' Jo!—
   Iry an' Billy's *the boys,*
   An' *Jo's* their *dog,* you know,—
Their pictur's took all in a row.
   Bet they kin kick up a noise—
   Iry an' Billy, the boys,
An' that-air little dog Jo!

Iry's the one 'at stands
   Up there a-lookin' so mild
An' meek—with his hat in his hands,
   Like such a *'bediant* child—
(*Sakes-alive!*)—An' *Billy* he sets
In the cheer an' holds on to Jo an' *sweats*
Hisse'f, a-lookin' so good! Ho-ho!
   Iry an' Billy an' Jo!

Yit the way them boys, you know,
    Usen to jes' turn in
An' fight over that dog Jo
    Wuz a burnin'-shame-an'-a-sin!—
Iry *he'd* argy 'at, by gee-whizz!
That-air little Jo-dog wuz *his!*—
An' Billy *he'd* claim it wuzn't so—
'Cause the dog wuz *hisn!*—An' at it they'd go,
Nip-an'-tugg, tooth-an'-toe-nail, you know—
    Iry an' Billy an' Jo!

But their Pa—(He wuz the marshal then)—
    He 'tended-like 'at he *jerked 'em up;*
An' got a jury o' Brick-yard men
    An' helt a *trial* about the pup:
An' *he* says *he* jes' like to 'a' died
When the rest o' us town-boys *testified*—
    Regardin', you know,
    Iry an' Billy an' Jo!

'Cause we all knowed, when *the Gipsies* they
    Camped down here by the crick last Fall,
They brung Jo with 'em, an' give him away
    To Iry an' Billy fer nothin' at all!—
So the jury fetched in the *verdick* so
    Jo he ain't *neether* o' theirn fer *shore*—
    He's *both* their dog, an' jes' no more!
    An' so
    They've quit quarrelin' long ago,
    Iry an' Billy an' Jo.

THE RUNAWAY BOY

WUNST I sassed my Pa, an' he
Won't stand that, an' punished me,—
Nen when he was gone that day,
I slipped out an' runned away.

I tooked all my copper-cents,
An' clumbed over our back fence
In the jimpson-weeds 'at growed
Ever'where all down the road.

Nen I got out there, an' nen
I runned some—an' runned again
When I met a man 'at led
A big cow 'at shooked her head.

I went down a long, long lane
Where was little pigs a-play'n';
An' a grea'-big pig went "Booh!"
An' jumped up, an' skeered me too.

Nen I scampered past, an' they
Was somebody hollered "Hey!"
An' I ist looked ever'where,
An' they was nobody there.

I *want* to, but I'm 'fraid to try
To go back. . . .An' by-an'-by,
Somepin' hurts my throat inside—
An' I want my Ma—an' cried.

Nen' a grea'-big girl come through
Where's a gate, an' telled me who
Am I? an' ef I tell where
My home's at she'll show me there.

But I couldn't ist but tell
What's my *name;* an' she says well,
An' she tooked me up an' says
She know where I live, she guess.

Nen she telled me hug wite close
Round her neck!—an' off she goes
Skippin' up the street! An' nen
Purty soon I'm home again.

An' my Ma, when she kissed me,
Kissed the *big girl* too, an' *she*
Kissed me—ef I p'omise *shore*
I won't run away no more!

BILLY MILLER'S CIRCUS-SHOW

AT Billy Miller's Circus-Show—
    In their old stable where it's at—
    The boys pays twenty pins to go,
  An' gits their money's-worth at that!—
'Cause Billy he can climb an' chalk
His stockin'-feet an' purt'-nigh walk
A tight-rope—yes, an' ef he fall
He'll ketch, an' "skin a cat"—'at's all!

He ain't afeard to swing an' hang
  Ist by his legs!—an' mayby stop
An' yell "Look out!" an' nen—k-spang!—
  He'll let loose, upside-down, an' drop
Wite on his hands! An' nen he'll do
"Contortion-acts"—ist limber through
As "Injarubber Mens" 'at goes
With shore-fer-certain circus-shows!

At Billy Miller's Circus-Show
    He's got a circus-ring—an' they's
A dressin'-room,—so's he can go
    An' dress an' paint up when he plays
He's somepin' else;—'cause sometimes he's
"Ringmaster"—bossin' like he please—
An' sometimes "Ephalunt"—er "Bare-
Back Rider," prancin' out o' there!

An' sometimes—an' the best of all!—
    He's "The Old Clown," an' got on clo'es
All stripud,—an' white hat, all tall
    An' peakud—like in shore-'nuff shows,—
An' got three-cornered red-marks, too,
On his white cheeks—ist like they do!—
An' you'd ist die, the way he sings
An' dances an' says funny things!

THE LAND OF USED-TO-BE

AND where's the Land of Used-to-be, does little
  baby wonder?
  Oh, we will clap a magic saddle over "Pop-
  um's" knee
And ride away around the world, and in and out
  and under
  The whole of all the golden sunny Summertime
  and see.

Leisurely and lazy-like we'll jostle on our journey,
  And let the pony bathe his hooves and cool them
    in the dew,
As he sidles down the shady way and lags along the
  ferny
  And green grassy edges of the lane we travel
  through.

And then we'll canter on to catch the bubble of the
      thistle
  As it bumps among the butterflies and glimmers
     down the sun,
To leave us laughing, all content to hear the robin
      whistle
  Or guess what Katydid is saying little Katy's done,

And pausing here a minute, where we hear the
      squirrel chuckle
  As he darts from out the underbrush and scampers
     up the tree,
We will gather buds and locust-blossoms, leaves and
      honeysuckle,
  To wreathe around our foreheads, riding into
     Used-to-be;—

For here's the very rim of it that we go swinging
      over—
  Don't you hear the Fairy bugles, and the tinkle of
     the bells,
And see the baby-bumblebees that tumble in the
      clover
  And dangle from the tilted pinks and tipsy pim-
     pernels?

And don't you see the merry faces of the daffodillies,
    And the jolly Johnny-jump-ups, and the buttercups
        a-glee,
And the low, lolling ripples ring around the water-
        lilies?—
    All greeting us with laughter, to the Land of
        Used-to-be!

And here among the blossoms of the blooming vines
        and grasses,
    With a haze forever hanging in a sky forever
        blue,
And with a breeze from over-seas to kiss us as it
        passes,
    We will romp around forever as the airy Elfins do!

For all the elves of earth and air are swarming here
        together—
    The prankish Puck, King Oberon, and Queen
        Titania too;
And dear old Mother Goose herself, as sunny as the
        weather,
    Comes dancing down the dewy walks to welcome
        me and you!

THE CLOVER

SOME sings of the lilly, and daisy, and rose,
And the pansies and pinks that the Summer-
time throws
In the green grassy lap of the medder that lays
Blinkin' up at the skyes through the sunshiny days;
But what is the lilly and all of the rest
Of the flowers, to a man with a hart in his brest
That was dipped brimmin' full of the honey and dew
Of the sweet clover-blossoms his babyhood knew?

I never set eyes on a clover-field now,
Er fool round a stable, er climb in the mow,
But my childhood comes back jest as clear and as plane
As the smell of the clover I'm sniffin' again;
And I wunder away in a barefooted dream,
Whare I tangle my toes in the blossoms that gleam
With the dew of the dawn of the morning of love
Ere it wept ore the graves that I'm weepin' above.

'And so I love clover—it seems like a part
Of the sacerdest sorrows and joys of my hart;
And wharever it blossoms, oh, thare let me bow
'And thank the good God as I'm thankin' Him now;
And I pray to Him still fer the stren'th when I die,
To go out in the clover and tell it good-by,
And lovin'ly nestle my face in its bloom
While my soul slips away on a breth of purfume.

OUT TO OLD AUNT MARY'S

WASN'T it pleasant, O brother mine,
In those old days of the lost sunshine
Of youth—When the Saturday's chores
were through,
And the "Sunday's wood" in the
kitchen, too,
And we went visiting, "me and you,"
Out to Old Aunt Mary's?—

"Me and you"—And the morning fair,
With the dewdrops twinkling everywhere;
The scent of the cherry-blossoms blown
After us, in the roadway lone,
Our capering shadows onward thrown—
Out to Old Aunt Mary's.

It all comes back so clear to-day!
Though I am as bald as you are gray,—
    Out by the barn-lot and down the lane
    We patter along in the dust again,
    As light as the tips of the drops of the rain,
            Out to Old Aunt Mary's.

The last few houses of the town;
Then on, up the high creek-bluffs and down;
    Past the squat toll-gate, with its well-sweep pole;
    The Bridge, and "the old 'babtizin'-hole,' "
    Loitering, awed, o'er pool and shoal,
            Out to Old Aunt Mary's.

We cross the pasture, and through the wood,
Where the old gray snag of the poplar stood,
    Where the hammering "red-heads" hopped awry,
    And the buzzard "raised" in the "clearing"-sky
    And lolled and circled, as we went by
            Out to Old Aunt Mary's.

Or, stayed by the glint of the redbird's wings,
Or the glitter of song that the bluebird sings,
    All hushed we feign to strike strange trails,
    As the "big braves" do in the Indian tales,
    Till again our real quest lags and fails—
            Out to Old Aunt Mary's.—

And the woodland echoes with yells of mirth
That make old war-whoops of minor worth! . . .
   Where such heroes of war as we?—
   With bows and arrows of fantasy,
   Chasing each other from tree to tree
      Out to Old Aunt Mary's!

And then in the dust of the road again;
And the teams we met, and the countrymen;
   And the long highway, with sunshine spread
   As thick as butter on country bread,
   Our cares behind, and our hearts ahead
      Out to Old Aunt Mary's.—

For only, now, at the road's next bend
To the right we could make out the gable-end
   Of the fine old Huston homestead—not
   Half a mile from the sacred spot
   Where dwelt our Saint in her simple cot—
      Out to Old Aunt Mary's.

Why, I see her now in the open door
Where the little gourds grew up the sides and o'er
   The clapboard roof!—And her face—ah, me!
   Wasn't it good for a boy to see—
   And wasn't it good for a boy to be
      Out to Old Aunt Mary's?—

The jelly—the jam and the marmalade,
And the cherry and quince "preserves" she made!
  And the sweet-sour pickles of peach and pear,
  With cinnamon in 'em and all things rare!—
  And the more we ate was the more to spare,
        Out to Old Aunt Mary's!

Ah, was there, ever, so kind a face
And gentle as hers, or such a grace
  Of welcoming, as she cut the cake
  Or the juicy pies that she joyed to make
  Just for the visiting children's sake—
        Out to Old Aunt Mary's!

The honey, too, in its amber comb
One only finds in an old farm-home;
  And the coffee, fragrant and sweet, and ho!
  So hot that we gloried to drink it so,
  With spangles of tears in our eyes, you know—
        Out to Old Aunt Mary's.

And the romps we took, in our glad unrest!—
Was it the lawn that we loved the best,
  With its swooping swing in the locust trees,
  Or was it the grove, with its leafy breeze,
  Or the dim haymow, with its fragrancies—
        Out to Old Aunt Mary's.

Far fields, bottom-lands, creek-banks—all,
We ranged at will.—Where the waterfall
    Laughed all day as it slowly poured
    Over the dam by the old mill-ford,
    While the tail-race writhed, and the mill-wheel
        roared—
            Out to Old Aunt Mary's.

But home, with Aunty in nearer call,
That was the best place, after all!—
    The talks on the back porch, in the low
    Slanting sun and the evening glow,
    With the voice of counsel that touched us so,
            Out to Old Aunt Mary's.

And then, in the garden—near the side
Where the beehives were and the path was wide,—
    The apple-house—like a fairy cell—
    With the little square door we knew so well,
    And the wealth inside but our tongues could tell—
            Out to Old Aunt Mary's.

And the old spring-house, in the cool green gloom
Of the willow trees,—and the cooler room
    Where the swinging shelves and the crocks were
        kept,
    Where the cream in a golden languor slept,
    While the waters gurgled and laughed and wept—
            Out to Old Aunt Mary's.

And as many a time have you and I—
Barefoot boys in the days gone by—
　　Knelt, and in tremulous ecstasies
　　Dipped our lips into sweets like these,—
　　Memory now is on her knees
　　　　　Out to Old Aunt Mary's.—

For, O my brother so far away,
This is to tell you—she waits *to-day*
　　To welcome us:—Aunt Mary fell
　　Asleep this morning, whispering, "Tell
　　The boys to come." . . . And all is well
　　　　　Out to Old Aunt Mary's.

THE OLD HAY-MOW

THE Old Hay-mow's the place to play
Fer boys, when it's a rainy day!
I good 'eal ruther be up there
Than down in town, er anywhere!

When I play in our stable-loft,
The good old hay's so dry an' soft,
An' feels so fine, an' smells so sweet,
I 'most ferget to go an' eat.

An' one time wunst I *did* ferget
To go 'tel dinner was all et,—
An' they had short-cake—an'—Bud he
Hogged up the piece Ma saved fer me

Nen I won't let him play no more
In our hay-mow where I keep store
An' got hen-eggs to sell,—an' shoo
The cackle-un old hen out, too!

An' nen, when Aunty she was here
A-visitun from Rensselaer,
An' bringed my little cousin,—*He*
Can come up there an' play with me.

But, after while—when Bud he bets
'At I can't turn no summersetts,—
I let him come up, ef he can
Ac' ha'f-way like a gentleman!

THE SQUIRT-GUN UNCLE MAKED ME

UNCLE SIDNEY, when he wuz here,
    Maked me a squirt-gun out o' some
    Elder-bushes 'at growed out near
Where wuz the brick-yard—'way out clear
    To where the Toll Gate come!

So when we walked back home again,
    He maked it, out in our woodhouse where
Wuz the old work-bench, an' the old jack-plane,
An' the old 'poke-shave, an' the tools all lay'n'
    Ist like he wants 'em there.

He sawed it first with the old hand-saw;
    An' nen he peeled off the bark, an' got
Some glass an' scraped it; an' told 'bout Pa,
When *he* wuz a boy an' fooled his Ma,
    An' the whippin' 'at he caught.

Nen Uncle Sidney, he took an' filed
    A' old arn ramrod; an' one o' the ends
He screwed fast into the vise; an' smiled,
Thinkin', he said, o' when he wuz a child,
    'Fore him an' Pa wuz mens.

He punched out the peth, an' nen he putt
    A plug in the end with a hole notched through;
Nen took the old drawey-knife an' cut
An' maked a handle 'at shoved clean shut
    But ist where yer hand held to.

An' he wropt th' uther end with some string an' white
    Piece o' the sleeve of a' old tored shirt;
An' nen he showed me to hold it tight,
An' suck in the water an' work it right—
    An' it 'ud ist squirt an' squirt!

THE BOYS' CANDIDATE

L AS' time 'at Uncle Sidney come,
He bringed a watermelon home—
    An' half the boys in town
Come taggin' after him.—An' he
Says, when we et it,—*"Gracious me!
'S the boy-house fell down?"*

LITTLE ORPHANT ANNIE

LITTLE Orphant Annie's come to our house to
stay,
An' wash the cups an' saucers up, an' bresh
the crumbs away,
An' shoo the chickens off the porch, an' dust the
hearth, an' sweep,
An' make the fire, an' bake the bread, an' earn her
board-an'-keep;
An' all us other childern, when the supper-things is
done,
We set around the kitchen fire an' has the mostest fun
A-list'nin' to the witch-tales 'at Annie tells about,
An' the Gobble-uns 'at gits you

   Ef you
    Don't
     Watch
      Out!

Onc't they was a little boy wouldn't say his prayers,—
So when he went to bed at night, away up stairs,
His Mammy heerd him holler, an' his Daddy heerd
      him bawl,
An' when they turn't the kivvers down, he wasn't
      there at all!
An' they seeked him in the rafter-room, an' cubby-
      hole, an' press,
An' seeked him up the chimbly-flue, an' ever'wheres,
      I guess;
But all they ever found was thist his pants an' round-
      about:—
An' the Gobble-uns'll git you
         Ef you
           Don't
             Watch
               Out!

An' one time a little girl 'ud allus laugh an' grin,
An' make fun of ever'one, an' all her blood an' kin;
An' onc't, when they was "company," an' ole folks
      was there,
She mocked 'em an' shocked 'em, an' said she didn't
      care!
An' thist as she kicked her heels, an' turn't to run an'
      hide,
They was two great big Black Things a-standin' by
      her side,

An' they snatched her through the ceilin' 'fore she
    knowed what she's about!
An' the Gobble-uns'll git you
            Ef you
                Don't
                    Watch
                        Out!

An' little Orphant Annie says when the blaze is blue,
An' the lamp-wick sputters, an' the wind goes *woo-oo!*
An' you hear the crickets quit, an' the moon is gray,
An' the lightnin'-bugs in dew is all squenched away,—
You better mind yer parunts an' yer teachers fond
        an' dear,
An' churish them 'at loves you, an' dry the orphant's
        tear,
An' he'p the pore an' needy ones 'at clusters all about,
Er the Gobble-uns'll git you
            Ef you
                Don't
                    Watch
                        Out!

A SONG OF LONG AGO

A SONG of Long Ago:
    Sing it lightly—sing it low—
    Sing it softly—like the lisping of the lips
       we used to know
When our baby-laughter spilled
From the glad hearts ever filled
With music blithe as robin ever trilled!

Let the fragrant summer breeze,
And the leaves of locust-trees,
And the apple-buds and -blossoms, and the wings of
      honey-bees,
All palpitate with glee,
Till the happy harmony
Brings back each childish joy to you and me.

Let the eyes of fancy turn
Where the tumbled pippins burn
Like embers in the orchard's lap of tangled grass and
      fern,—
There let the old path wind
In and out, and on behind
The cider-press that chuckles as we grind.

Blend in the song the moan
Of the dove that grieves alone,
And the wild whir of the locust, and the bumble's
        drowsy drone;
And the low of cows that call
Through the pasture-bars when all
The landscape fades away at evenfall.

Then, far away and clear,
Through the dusky atmosphere,
Let the wailing of the killdee be the only sound we hear:
O sad and sweet and low
As the memory may know
Is the glad-pathetic song of Long Ago!

BILLY AND HIS DRUM

HO! it's come, kids, come!
With a bim! bam! bum!
Here's little Billy bangin' on
    his big bass drum!
He's a-marchin' round the room,
With his feather-duster plume
A-noddin' an' a-bobbin' with his
    bim! bam! boom!

Looky, little Jane an' Jim!
Will you only look at him,
A-humpin' an' a-thumpin' with his
    bam! bom! bim!
Has the Day o' Judgment come
Er the New Mi-len-nee-um?
Er is it only Billy with his
    bim! bam! bum!

I'm a-comin'; yes, I am—
Jim an' Sis, an' Jane an' Sam!
We'll all march off with Billy and his
    bom! bim! bam!
Come hur*raw*in' as you come,
Er they'll think you're deef-an'-dumb
Ef you don't hear little Billy an' his
    big bass drum!

THE BOY LIVES ON OUR FARM

THE Boy lives on our Farm, he's not
    Afeard o' horses none!
    An' he can make 'em lope, er trot,
Er rack, er pace, er run.
Sometimes he drives two horses, when
    He comes to town an' brings
A wagon-full o' 'taters nen,
    An' roastin'-ears an' things.

Two horses is "a team," he says,—
    An' when you drive er hitch,
The right-un's a "near-horse," I guess,
    Er "off"—I don't know which.—
The Boy lives on our Farm, he told
    Me, too, 'at he can see,
By lookin' at their teeth, how old
    A horse is, to a T!

I'd be the gladdest boy alive
   Ef I knowed much as that,
An' could stand up like him an' drive,
   An' ist push back my hat,
Like he comes skallyhootin' through
   Our alley, with one arm
A-wavin' Fare-ye-well! to you—
   The Boy lives on our Farm!

GOIN' TO THE FAIR
OLD STYLE

WHEN Me an' my Ma an' Pa went to the Fair,
Ma borried Mizz Rollins-uz rigg to go there,
'Cause *our* buggy's *new,* an' Ma says, "Mercy-
sake!
It wouldn't hold *half* the folks *she's* go' to take!"
An' she took Marindy, an' Jane's twins, an' Jo,
An' Aunty Van Meters-uz girls—an' old Slo'
Magee, 'at's so fat, come a-scrougin' in there,
When me an' my Ma an' Pa went to the Fair!

The road's full o' loads-full 'ist ready to bu'st,
An' all hot, an' smokin' an' chokin' with dust;
The Wolffs an' their wagon, an' Brizentines, too—
An' horses 'ist r'ared when the toot-cars come through!
An' 'way from fur off we could hear the band play,
An' peoples all there 'u'd 'ist whoop an' hooray!
An' I stood on the dashboard, an' Pa boost' me there
'Most high as the fence, when we went to the Fair.

An' when we uz there an' inside, we could see
Wher' the flag's on a pole wher' a show's go' to be;
An' boys up in trees, an' the grea'-big balloon
'At didn't goned up a-tall, all afternoon!
An' a man in the crowd there gived money away—
An' Pa says *"he'd* ruther earn *his* by the day!"—
An' *he* gim-me some, an' says "ain't nothin' there
Too good fer his boy," when we went to the Fair.

Wisht the Raggedy Man wuz there, too!—but he says,
"Don't talk fairs to *me*, child! I went to one;—yes,—
An' there wuz a swing there ye rode—an' I rode,
An' a thing-um-a-jing 'at ye blowed—an' I blowed;
An' they wuz a game 'at ye played—an' I played,
An' a hitch in the same wher' ye paid—an' I paid;
An' they wuz *two* bad to one good peoples there—
Like *you* an' your *Pa* an' Ma went to the Fair!"

THE DOODLE BUGS'S CHARM

WHEN Uncle Sidney he comes here—
      An' Fred an' me an' Min,—
      My Ma she says she bet you yet
The roof'll tumble in!
For Uncle he ist *romps* with us:
  An' wunst, out in our shed,
He telled us 'bout the Doodle-Bugs,
  An' what they'll do, he said,
Ef you'll ist holler "Doodle-Bugs!"—
  Out by our garden-bed—
"Doodle-Bugs! Doodle-Bugs!
  Come up an' git some bread!"

Ain't Uncle Sidney funny man?—
    "He's childish 'most as me"—
My Ma sometimes she tells him that—
    "He ac's so foolishly!"
W'y, wunst, out in our garden-path
    Wite by the pie-plant bed,
He all sprawled out there in the dirt
    An' ist scrooched down his head,
An' "Doodle! Doodle! Doodle-Bugs!"
    My Uncle Sidney said,—
"Doodle-Bugs! Doodle-Bugs!
    Come up an' git some bread!"

An' nen he showed us little holes
    All bored there in the ground,
An' little weenty heaps o' dust
    'At's piled there all around:
An' Uncle said, when he's like us,
    Er purt' nigh big as Fred,
That wuz the Doodle-Bugs's Charm—
    To call 'em up, he said:—
"Doodle! Doodle! Doodle-Bugs!"
    An' they'd poke out their head—
"Doodle-Bugs! Doodle-Bugs!
    Come up an' git some bread!"

MISTER HOP-TOAD

HOWDY, Mister Hop-Toad! Glad to see you out!
Bin a month o' Sund'ys sense I seen you here-
about.
Kind o' bin a-layin' in, from the frost and snow?
Good to see you out ag'in, it's bin so long ago!
Plow's like slicin' cheese, and sod's loppin' over even;
Loam's like gingerbread, and clod's softer'n deceivin'—
Mister Hop-Toad, honest-true—Spring-time—don't you
love it?
You old rusty rascal you, at the bottom of it!

Oh! oh! oh!
I grabs up my old hoe;
But I sees *you,*
And s' I, "Ooh-ooh!
Howdy, Mister Hop-Toad! How-dee-do!"

Make yourse'f more comfo'bler—square 'round at your
    ease—
Don't set saggin' slanchwise, with your nose below your
    knees.
Swell that fat old throat o' yourn and lemme see you
    swaller;
Straighten up and h'ist your head!—*You* don't owe a
    dollar!—
Hain't no mor'gage on your land—ner no taxes, nuther;
You don't haf to work no roads, even ef you'd ruther.
'F I was you, and *fixed* like you, I really wouldn't keer
To swap fer life and hop right in the presidential cheer!

Oh! oh! oh!
I hauls back my old hoe;
But I sees *you,*
And s' I, "Ooh-ooh!
Howdy, Mister Hop-Toad! How-dee-do!"

'Long about next Aprile, hoppin' down the furry,
Won't you mind I ast you what 'peared to be the hurry?—
Won't you mind I hooked my hoe and hauled you back
    and smiled?—
W'y, bless you, Mister Hop-Toad, I love you like a child!
S'pose I'd want to 'flict you any more'n what you air?—
S'pose I think you got no rights 'cept the warts you wear?

Hulk, sulk, and blink away, you old bloat-eyed rowdy!—
Hain't you got a word to say?—Won't you tell me
"Howdy"?

   Oh! oh! oh!
   I swish round my old hoe;
   But I sees *you,*
   And s' I, "Ooh-ooh!
Howdy, Mister Hop-Toad! How-dee-do!"

OUR HIRED GIRL

OUR hired girl, she's 'Lizabuth Ann;
    An' she can cook best things to eat!
  She ist puts dough in our pie-pan,
  An' pours in somepin' 'at's good and sweet,
An' nen she salts it all on top
With cinnamon; an' nen she'll stop
  An' stoop an' slide it, ist as slow,
In th' old cook-stove, so's 'twon't slop
  An' git all spilled; nen bakes it, so
  It's custard pie, first thing you know!
    An' nen she'll say:
  "Clear out o' my way!
  They's time fer work, an' time fer play!—
    Take yer dough, an' run, Child; run!
    Er I cain't git no cookin' done!"

When our hired girl 'tends like she's mad,
  An' says folks got to walk the chalk
When *she's* around, er wisht they had,
  I play out on our porch an' talk
To th' Raggedy Man 'at mows our lawn;
  An' he says *"Whew!"* an' nen leans on
  His old crook-scythe, and blinks his eyes
An' sniffs all round an' says,—"I swawn!
  Ef my old nose don't tell me lies,
  It 'pears like I smell custard-pies!"
    An' nen *he'll* say,—
  "'Clear out o' my way!
  They's time fer work an' time fer play!
    Take yer dough, an' run, Child; run!
    Er *she* cain't git no cookin' done!'"

Wunst our hired girl, when she
  Got the supper, an' we all et,
An' it was night, an' Ma an' me
  An' Pa went wher' the "Social" met,—
An' nen when we come home, an' see
A light in the kitchen-door, an' we
  Heerd a maccordeun, Pa says "Lan'-
O'-Gracious! who can *her* beau be?"

An' I marched in, an' 'Lizabuth Ann
Wuz parchin' corn fer the Raggedy Man!
   Better say
"Clear out o' the way!
They's time fer work, an' time fer play!
  Take the hint, an' run, Child; run!
  Er we cain't git no *courtin'* done!"

WHEN EARLY MARCH SEEMS MIDDLE MAY

WHEN country roads begin to thaw
    In mottled spots of damp and dust,
    And fences by the margin draw
  Along the frosty crust
Their graphic silhouettes, I say,
The Spring is coming round this way.

When morning-time is bright with sun
  And keen with wind, and both confuse
The dancing, glancing eyes of one
  With tears that ooze and ooze—
And nose-tips weep as well as they,
The Spring is coming round this way.

When suddenly some shadow-bird
  Goes wavering beneath the gaze,
And through the hedge the moan is heard
  Of kine that fain would graze
In grasses new, I smile and say,
The Spring is coming round this way.

When knotted horse-tails are untied,
  And teamsters whistle here and there,
And clumsy mitts are laid aside
  And choppers' hands are bare,

And chips are thick where children play,
The Spring is coming round this way.

When through the twigs the farmer tramps,
   And troughs are chunked beneath the trees,
And fragrant hints of sugar-camps
   Astray in every breeze,—
When early March seems middle May,
The Spring is coming round this way.

When coughs are changed to laughs, and when
   Our frowns melt into smiles of glee,
And all our blood thaws out again
   In streams of ecstasy,
And poets wreak their roundelay,
The Spring is coming round this way.

THE TOY-BALLOON

THEY wuz a Big Day wunst in town,
    An' little Jason's Pa
    Buyed him a little toy-balloon,
The first he ever saw.—
An' oh! but Jase wuz *more'n* proud,
    A-holdin' to the string
An' scrougin' threugh the grea'-big crowd,
    To hear the Glee Club sing.

The Glee Club it wuz goin' to sing
    In old Masonic Hall;
An' Speakin', it wuz in there, too,
    An' soldiers, folks an' all,
An' Jason's Pa he git a seat
    An' set down purty soon,
A-holdin' little Jase, an' him
    A-holdin' his balloon.

An' while the Speakin' 's startin' up
    An' ever'body still—
The first you know wuz little Jase
    A-yellin' fit to kill!—
Nen Jason's Pa jump on his seat
    An' grab up in the air,—
But little Jason's toy-balloon
    Wuz clean away from there!

An' Jase he yelled; an' Jase's Pa,
    Still lookin' up, clumb down—
While that-air little toy-balloon
    Went bumpin' roun' an' roun'
Ag'inst the ceilin', 'way up there
    Where ever'body saw,
An' *they* all yelled, an' *Jason* yelled
    An' little Jason's Pa!

But when his Pa he packed him out
    A-screamin'—nen the crowd
Looked down an' hushed—till they looked up
    An' howled ag'in out loud;
An' nen the speaker, mad an' pale,
    Jist turned an' left the stand,
An' all j'ined in the Glee Club—"Hail,
    Columby, Happy Land!"

THE BOY PATRIOT

I WANT to be a Soldier!—
A Soldier!—
A Soldier!—
I want to be a Soldier, with a saber in my hand
Or a little carbine rifle, or a musket on my shoulder,
Or just a snare-drum, snarling in the middle of the band;
I want to hear, high overhead, The Old Flag flap her
wings
While all the Army, following, in chorus cheers and
sings;
I want to hear the tramp and jar
Of patriots a million,
As gaily dancing off to war
As dancing a cotillion.

I want to be a Soldier!—
A Soldier!—
A Soldier!—
I want to be a Soldier, with a saber in my hand
Or a little carbine rifle, or a musket on my shoulder,
Or just a snare-drum, snarling in the middle of the band.

I want to see the battle!—

The battle!—

The battle!—

I want to see the battle, and be in it to the end;—

I want to hear the cannon clear their throats and catch the
prattle

Of all the pretty compliments the enemy can send!—

And then I know my wits will go,—and where I *shouldn't*
be—

Well, there's the spot, in any fight, that you may search
for me.

So, when our foes have had their fill,
Though I'm among the dying,
To see The Old Flag flying still,
I'll laugh to leave her flying!

I want to be a Soldier!—

A Soldier!—

A Soldier!—

I want to be a Soldier, with a saber in my hand
Or a little carbine rifle, or a musket on my shoulder,
Or just a snare-drum, snarling in the middle of the band.

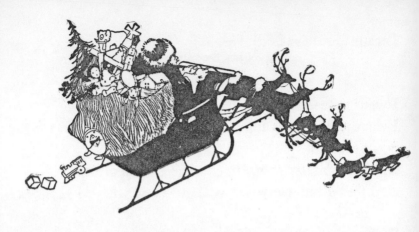

WHAT LITTLE SAUL GOT FOR CHRISTMAS

US PARENTS mostly thinks our own's
    The smartest childern out!
    But widder Shelton's little Saul
Beats all *I* know about!
He's weakly-like—in p'int o' *health*,
    But strong in word and deed
And heart and head, and snap and spunk,
    And allus in the lead!

Come honest' by it, fer his Pa—
    Afore he passed away—
He was a leader—(Lord, I'd like
    To hear him preach to-day!)
He led *his* flock; he led in prayer
    Fer spread o' Peace—and when
Nothin' but *War* could spread it, he
    Was first to lead us *then!*

So little Saul has grit to take
  Things jes as they occur;
And sister Shelton's proud o' him
  As he is proud o' her!
And when she "got up"—jes fer him
  And little playmates all—
A Chris'mus-tree,—they ever'one
  Was there but little Saul.—

Pore little chap was sick in bed
  Next room; and Doc was there,
And said the childern might file past,
  But go right back to where
The *tree* was, in the settin'-room.
  And Saul jes laid and smiled—
Ner couldn't nod, ner wave his hand,
  It hurt so—Bless the child!

And so they left him there with Doc—
  And warm tear of his Ma's. . . . .
Then—suddent-like—high over all
  Their laughture and applause—
They heerd,—"I don't care *what* you git
  On yer old Chris'mus-tree,
'Cause *I'm* got somepin' *you* all haint,—
  I'm got the pleurisy!"

THE ALL-GOLDEN

I

THROUGH every happy line I sing
I feel the tonic of the Spring.
The day is like an old-time face
That gleams across some grassy place—
An old-time face—an old-time chum
Who rises from the grave to come
And lure me back along the ways
Of time's all-golden yesterdays.
Sweet day! to thus remind me of
The truant boy I used to love—
To set, once more, his finger-tips
Against the blossom of his lips,
And pipe for me the signal known
By none but him and me alone!

II

I see, across the schoolroom floor,
The shadow of the open door,
And dancing dust and sunshine blent
Slanting the way the morning went,
And beckoning my thoughts afar
Where reeds and running waters are;

Where amber-colored bayous glass
The half-drown'd weeds and wisps of grass,
Where sprawling frogs, in loveless key,
Sing on and on incessantly.
Against the green wood's dim expanse
The cattail tilts its tufted lance,
While on its tip—one might declare
The white "snake-feeder" blossomed there!

III

I catch my breath, as children do
In woodland swings when life is new,
And all the blood is warm as wine
And tingles with a tang divine.
My soul soars up the atmosphere
And sings aloud where God can hear,
And all my being leans intent
To mark His smiling wonderment.
O gracious dream, and gracious time,
And gracious theme, and gracious rhyme—
When buds of Spring begin to blow
In blossoms that we used to know
And lure us back along the ways
Of time's all-golden yesterdays!

NAUGHTY CLAUDE

WHEN Little Claude was naughty wunst
　　At dinner-time, an' said
　　He won't say *"Thank you"* to his Ma,
She maked him go to bed
An' stay two hours an' not git up,—
　　So when the clock struck Two,
Nen Claude says,—"Thank you, Mr. Clock,
　　I'm much obleeged to you!"

LITTLE MANDY'S CHRISTMAS-TREE

LITTLE Mandy and her Ma
'S porest folks you ever saw!—
Lived in porest house in town,
Where the fence 'uz all tore down.

And no front-door steps at all—
Ist a' old box 'g'inst the wall;
And no door-knob on the door
Outside.—*My!* but they 'uz pore!

Wuz no winder-shutters on,
And some of the *winders* gone,
And where *they* 'uz broke they'd pas'e
Ist brown paper 'crost the place.

Tell you! when it's *winter there,*
And the snow ist ever'where,
Little Mandy's Ma she say
'Spec' they'll freeze to death some day.

Wunst my Ma and me—when we
Be'n to church, and's goin' to be
Chris'mus purty soon,—we went
There—like the Committee sent.

And-sir! when we're in the door,
Wuz no carpet on the floor,
And no fire—and heels-and-head
Little Mandy's tucked in bed!

And her Ma told *my* Ma she
Got no coffee but ist tea,
And fried mush—and's all they had
Sence her health broke down so bad.

Nen Ma hug and hold me where
Little Mandy's layin' there;
And she kiss her, too, and nen
Mandy kiss my Ma again.

And my Ma she told her *we*
Goin' to have a Chris'mus-Tree,
At the Sund'y School, 'at's fer
ALL the childern, and fer *her.*

Little Mandy *think*—nen she
Say, "What *is* a Chris'mus-Tree?" .
Nen my Ma she gived *her* Ma
Somepin' 'at I never saw,

And say she *must* take it,—and
She ist maked her keep her hand
Wite close shut,—and nen she *kiss*
Her hand—shut ist like it is.

Nen we comed away. . . . 'And nen
When it's Chris'mus Eve again,
And all of us childerns be
At the Church and Chris'mus-Tree—

And all git our toys and things
'At old Santy Claus he brings
And puts on the Tree;—wite where
The *big* Tree 'uz standin' there,

And the things 'uz all tooked down,
And the childerns, all in town,
Got their presents—nen we see
They's a *little* Chris'mus-Tree

Wite *behind* the *big* Tree—so
We can't see till *nen,* you know,—
And it's all ist loaded down
With the purtiest things in town!

And the teacher smile and say:
"This-here Tree 'at's hid away
It's marked *'Little Mandy's Tree.'*
Little Mandy! Where is she?"

Nen nobody say a word.—
Stillest place you ever heard!—
Till a man tiptoe up where
Teacher's still a-waitin' there.

Nen the man he whispers, so
Ist the *Teacher* hears, you know.
Nen he tiptoe back and go
Out the big door—ist as slow!

. . . . .

Little Mandy, though, *she* don't
Answer—and Ma say "she won't
Never, though each year they'll be
'Little Mandy's Chris'mus-Tree'

Fer pore childern"—my Ma says
And *Committee* say they guess
"Little Mandy's Tree" 'ull be
Bigger than the *other* Tree!

WET-WEATHER TALK

IT hain't no use to grumble and complane;
   It's jest as cheap and easy to rejoice.—
   When God sorts out the weather and sends rain,
W'y, rain's my choice.

Men ginerly, to all intents—
   Although they're apt to grumble some—
Puts most theyr trust in Providence,
   And takes things as they come—
     That is, the commonality
     Of men that's lived as long as me
     Has watched the world enugh to learn
     They're not the boss of this concern.

With *some*, of course, it's different—
   I've saw *young* men that knowed it all,
And didn't like the way things went
   On this terrestchul ball;—
     But all the same, the rain, some way,
     Rained jest as hard on picnic day;
     Er, when they railly *wanted* it,
     It mayby wouldn't rain a bit!

In this existunce, dry and wet
   Will overtake the best of men—
Some little skift o' clouds'll shet
   The sun off now and then.—

And mayby, whilse you're wundern who
You've fool-like lent your umbrell' to,
And *want* it—out'll pop the sun,
And you'll be glad you hain't got none!

It aggervates the farmers, too—
    They's too much wet, er too much sun,
Er work, er waitin' round to do
    Before the plowin' 's done:
        And mayby, like as not, the wheat,
        Jest as it's lookin' hard to beat,
        Will ketch the storm—and jest about
        The time the corn's a-jintin' out.

These-here *cy-clones* a-foolin' round—
    And back'ard crops!—and wind and rain!—
And yit the corn that's wallerd down
    May elbow up again!—
        They hain't no sense, as I can see,
        Fer mortuls, sich as us, to be
        A-faultin' Natchur's wise intents,
        And lockin' horns with Providence!

It hain't no use to grumble and complane;
    It's jest as cheap and easy to rejoice.—
When God sorts out the weather and sends rain,
    W'y, rain's my choice.

THE LAND OF THUS-AND-SO

"HOW would Willie like to go
To the Land of Thus-and-So?
Everything is proper there—
All the children comb their hair
Smoother than the fur of cats,
Or the nap of high silk hats;
Every face is clean and white
As a lily washed in light;
Never vaguest soil or speck
Found on forehead, throat or neck;
Every little crimpled ear,
In and out, as pure and clear
As the cherry-blossom's blow
In the Land of Thus-and-So.

"Little boys that never fall
Down the stair, or cry at all—
Doing nothing to repent,
Watchful and obedient;
Never hungry, nor in haste—
Tidy shoe-strings always laced;
Never button rudely torn
From its fellows all unworn;
Knickerbockers always new—
Ribbon, tie, and collar, too;
Little watches, worn like men,
Always promptly half-past ten—
Just precisely right, you know,
For the Land of Thus-and-So!

"And the little babies there
Give no one the slightest care—
Nurse has not a thing to do
But be happy and sigh 'Boo!'
While Mamma just nods, and knows
Nothing but to doze and doze:
Never litter round the grate;
Never lunch or dinner late;
Never any household din
Peals without or rings within—
Baby coos nor laughing calls
On the stairs or through the halls—
Just Great Hushes to and fro
Pace the Land of Thus-and-so!

"Oh! the Land of Thus-and-So!—
Isn't it delightful, though?"
"Yes," lisped Willie, answering **me**
Somewhat slow and doubtfully—
"Must be awful nice, but I
Ruther wait till by-and-by
'Fore I go there—maybe when
I be dead I'll go there *then.*—
But"—the troubled little face
Closer pressed in my embrace—
"Le's don't never *ever* go
To the Land of Thus-and-So!"

AT AUNTY'S HOUSE

ONE time, when we'z at Aunty's house—
    'Way in the country!—where
    They's ist but woods—an' pigs, an' cows—
An' all's outdoors an' air!—
An' orchurd-swing; an' churry-trees—
An' *churries* in 'em!—Yes, an' these-
Here redhead birds steals all they please,
    An' tetch 'em ef you dare!—
W'y, wunst, one time, when we wuz there,
    We et out on the porch!

Wite where the cellar-door wuz shut
　　The table wuz; an' I
Let Aunty set by me an' cut
　　My vittuls up—an' pie.
'Tuz awful funny!—I could see
The redheads in the churry-tree,
An' beehives, where you got to be
　　So keerful, goin' by;—
An' "Comp'ny" there an' all!—an' we—
　　We et out on the porch!

An' I ist et *p'surves* an' things
　　'At Ma don't 'low me to—
An' *chicken-gizzurds*—(don't like *wings*
　　Like *Parunts* does! do *you?*)
An' all the time the wind blowed there,
An' I could feel it in my hair,
An' ist smell clover *ever*'where!—
　　An' a' old redhead flew
Purt'-nigh wite over my high-chair,
　　When we et on the porch!

LITTLE JOHNTS'S CHRIS'MUS

WE got it up a-purpose, jes fer little Johnts,
    you know;
    His mother was so pore an' all, an' had
    to manage so—
Jes bein' a War-widder, an' her pension mighty slim,
She'd take in weavin', er work out, er anything, fer
    him!

An' little Johnts was puny-like, but law, *the nerve* he
    had!—
You'd want to kindo' pity him, but couldn't, very
    bad,—
His pants o' army-blanket an' his coat o' faded blue
Kep' hintin' of his father, like, an' pity wouldn't do!

So we collogued together, onc't, one winter-time, 'at
    we—
Jes me an' mother an' the girls, an' Wilse, John-Jack
    an' Free—
Would jine an' git up little Johnts, by time 'at
    Chris'mus come,
Some sort o' doin's, don't you know, 'at would
    su'prise him some.

An' so, all on the quiet, Mother she turns in an' gits
Some blue-janes—cuts an' makes a suit; an' then sets
      down an' knits
A pair o' little galluses to go 'long with the rest—
An' putts in a red-flannen back, an' buckle on the
       vest.—

The little feller'd be'n so much around our house,
      you see,
An' be'n sich he'p to her an' all, an' handy as could be,
'At Mother couldn't do too much fer little Johnts—
      No, *Sir!*
She ust to jes declare 'at "he was meat-an'-drink to
      her!"

An' Piney, Lide, an' Madaline they watched their
      chance an' rid
To Fountaintown with Lijey's folks; an' bought a
      book, they did,
O' fairy tales, with pictur's in; an' got a little pair
O' red-top boots 'at John-Jack said he'd be'n a-pricin'
      there.

An' Lide got him a little sword, an' Madaline, a
      drum;
An' shootin'-crackers—Lawzy-day! an' they're so
      dangersome!

An' Piney, ever' time the rest 'ud buy some other
       toy,
She'd take an' turn in then an' buy more candy fer
       the boy!

"Well," thinks-says-I, when they got back, *"your*
       pocketbooks is dry!"—
But little Johnts was there hisse'f that afternoon,
       so I—
Well, *all* of us kep' mighty mum, tel we got him
       away
By tellin' him be shore an' come to-morry—Chris'-
       mus Day—

An' fetch *his mother* 'long with him! An' how he
       scud acrost
The fields—his towhead, in the dusk, jes like a
       streak o' frost!—
His comfort fluttern as he run—an' old Tige, don't
       you know,
A-jumpin' high fer rabbits an' a ploughin' up the
       snow!

It must 'a' be'n 'most *ten* that night afore we got
       to bed—
With Wilse an' John-Jack he'pin' us; an' Freeman
       in the shed,

An' Lide out with the lantern while he trimmed the
　　　Chris'mus-Tree
Out of a little scrub-oak-top 'at suited to a "T"!

All night I dreamp' o' hearin' things a-skulkin'
　　　round the place—
An' "Old Kriss," with his whiskers off, an' freckles
　　　on his face—
An' reindeers, shaped like shavin'-hosses at the
　　　cooper-shop,
A-stickin' down the chimbly, with their heels out at
　　　the top!

By time 'at Mother got me up 'twas plum' daylight
　　　an' more—
The front yard full o' neighbers all a-crowdin' round
　　　the door,
With Johnts's mother leadin'; yes—an' little Johnts
　　　hisse'f,
Set up on Freeman's shoulder, like a jug up on the
　　　she'f!

Of course I can't describe it when they all got in
　　　to where
We'd conjered up the Chris'mus-Tree an' all the
　　　fixin's there!—
Fer all the shouts o' laughture—clappin' hands, an'
　　　crackin' jokes,
Was heap o' kissin' goin' on amongst the women-
　　　folks:—

Fer, lo-behold-ye! there they had that young-un!—
　　An' his chin
A-wobblin'-like;—an', shore enough, at last he
　　started in—
An'—sich another bellerin', in all my mortal days,
I never heerd, er 'spect to hear, in woe's app'inted
　　ways!

An' Mother grabs him up an' says: "It's more'n he
　　can bear—
It's all too *suddent* fer the child, an' too su'prisin'!
　　—*There!*"
"Oh, no it ain't"—sobbed little Johnts—"I ain't
　　su'prised—but I'm
A-cryin' 'cause I watched you all, an' knowed it all
　　the time!"

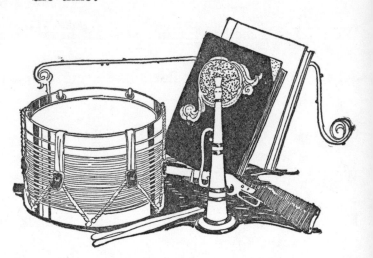

OUR KIND OF A MAN

I

THE kind of a man for you and me!
    He faces the world unflinchingly,
      And smites, as long as the wrong resists,
With a knuckled faith and force like fists:
He lives the life he is preaching of,
And loves where most is the need of love;
His voice is clear to the deaf man's ears,
And his face sublime through the blind man's tears;
The light shines out where the clouds were dim,
And the widow's prayer goes up for him;
The latch is clicked at the hovel door
And the sick man sees the sun once more,
And out o'er the barren fields he sees
Springing blossoms and waving trees,
Feeling as only the dying may,
That God's own servant has come that way,
Smoothing the path as it still winds on
Through the golden gate where his loved have gone.

The kind of a man for me and you!
However little of worth we do
He credits full, and abides in trust
That time will teach us how more is just.
He walks abroad, and he meets all kinds
Of querulous and uneasy minds,
And, sympathizing, he shares the pain
Of the doubts that rack us, heart and brain;
And, knowing this, as we grasp his hand,
We are surely coming to understand!
He looks on sin with pitying eyes—
E'en as the Lord, since Paradise,—
Else, should we read, Though our sins should glow
As scarlet, they shall be white as snow?—
And, feeling still, with a grief half glad,
That the bad are as good as the good are bad,
He strikes straight out for the Right—and he
Is the kind of a man for you and me!

WHEN THE WORLD BU'STS THROUGH

WHERE'S a boy a-goin',
　　An' what's he goin' to do,
　　An' how's he goin' to do it,
　When the world bu'sts through?
Ma she says "she can't tell
　What we're comin' to!"
An' Pop says "he's ist skeered
　Clean—plum—through!"

S'pose we'd be a-playin'
　Out in the street,
An' the ground 'ud split up
　'Bout forty feet!—
Ma says "she ist knows
　We 'ud tumble in";
An' Pop says "he bets you
　Nen we wouldn't grin!"

S'pose we ist be 'tendin'
  Like we had a show,
Down in the stable,
  Where we mustn't go,—
Ma says, "The earthquake
  Might make it fall";
'An' Pop says, "More'n like
  Swaller barn an' all!"

Landy! ef we both wuz
  Runnin' 'way from school,
Out in the shady woods
  Where it's all so cool!—
Ma says "a big tree
  Might sqush our head";
'An' Pop says, "Chop 'em out
  Both—killed—dead!"

But where's a boy goin',
  And what's he goin' to do,
'An' how's he goin' to do it,
  Ef the world bu'sts through?
Ma she says "she can't tell
  What we're comin' to!"
'An' Pop says "he's ist skeered
  Clean—plum—through!"

THE BEAR STORY

THAT ALEX "IST MAKED UP HIS-OWN-SE'F"

W'Y, wunst they wuz a Little Boy went out
  In the woods to shoot a Bear. So, he
          went out
'Way in the grea'-big woods—he did.—An' he
Wuz goin' along—an' goin' along, you know,
An' purty soon he heerd somepin' go *"Wooh!"*—
Ist thataway—*"Woo-ooh!"* An' he wuz *skeered,*
He wuz. An' so he runned an' clumbed a tree—
A grea'-big tree, he did,—a sicka-*more* tree.
An' nen he heerd it ag'in: an' he looked round,
An' *'t'uz a Bear!—a grea'-big shore-nuff Bear!*—
No: 't'uz *two* Bears, it wuz—two grea'-big Bears—
One of 'em wuz—ist *one'z* a *grea'-big* Bear.—
But they ist *boff* went *"Wooh!"*—An' here *they* come
To climb the tree an' git the Little Boy
An' eat him up!

            An' nen the Little Boy
He 'uz skeered worse'n ever! An' here come

The grea'-big Bear a-climbin' th' tree to git
The Little Boy an' eat him up—Oh, *no!*—
It 'uzn't the *Big* Bear 'at clumb the tree—
It 'uz the *Little* Bear. So here *he* come
Climbin' the tree—an' climbin' the tree! Nen when
He git wite *clos't* to the Little Boy, w'y nen
The Little Boy he ist pulled up his gun
An' *shot* the Bear, he did, an' killed him dead!
An' nen the Bear he falled clean on down out
The tree—away clean to the ground, he did—
Spling-splung! he falled *plum'* down, an' killed him,
    too!
An' lit wite side o' where the *Big* Bear's at.

An' nen the Big Bear's awful mad, you bet!—
'Cause—'cause the Little Boy he shot his gun
An' killed the *Little* Bear.—'Cause the *Big* Bear
He—he 'uz the Little Bear's Papa.—An' so here
He come to climb the big old tree an' git
The Little Boy an' eat him up! An' when
The Little Boy he saw the *grea'-big Bear*
A-comin', he 'uz badder skeered, he wuz,
Than *any* time! An' so he think he'll climb
Up *higher*—'way up higher in the tree
Than the old *Bear* kin climb, you know.—But he
He *can't* climb higher 'an old *Bears* kin climb,—
'Cause Bears kin climb up higher in the trees
Than any little Boys in all the Wo-r-r-ld!

An' so here come the grea'-big Bear, he did,—
A-climbin' up—an' up the tree, to git
The Little Boy an' eat him up! An' so
The Little Boy he clumbed on higher, an' higher,
An' higher up the tree—an' higher—an' higher—
An' higher'n iss-here *house* is!—An' here come
Th' old Bear—clos'ter to him all the time!—
An' nen—first thing you know,—when th' old Big
       Bear
Wuz wite clos't to him—nen the Little Boy
Ist jabbed his gun wite in the old Bear's mouf
An' shot an' killed him dead!—No; I *fergot,*—
He didn't shoot the grea'-big Bear at all—
'Cause *they 'uz no load in the gun,* you know—
'Cause when he shot the *Little* Bear, w'y, nen
No load 'uz anymore nen *in* the gun!

But th' Little Boy clumbed *higher* up, he did—
He clumbed *lots* higher—an' on up *higher*—an' higher
An' *higher*—tel he ist *can't* climb no higher,
'Cause nen the limbs 'uz all so little, 'way
Up in the teeny-weeny tip-top of
The tree, they'd break down wiv him ef he don't
Be keerful! So he stop an' think: An' nen
He look around—*An' here come th' old Bear!*

An' so the Little Boy make up his mind
He's got to ist git out o' there *some* way!—

'Cause here come the old Bear!—so clos't, his bref's
Purt' nigh so's he kin feel how hot it is
Ag'inst his bare feet—ist like old "Ring's" bref
When he's ben out a-huntin' an's all tired.
So when th' old Bear's so clos't—the Little Boy
Ist gives a grea'-big jump fer *'nother* tree—
No!—no he don't do that!—I tell you what
The Little Boy does:—W'y, nen—w'y, he—Oh, *yes*—
The Little Boy *he finds a hole up there*
'At's in the tree—an' climbs in there an' *hides*—
An' *nen* th' old Bear can't find the Little Boy
At all!—But, purty soon th' old Bear finds
The Little Boy's *gun* 'at's up there—'cause the *gun*
It's too *tall* to tooked wiv him in the hole.
So, when the old Bear fin' the *gun,* he knows
The Little Boy's ist *hid* 'round *somers* there,—
An' th' old Bear 'gins to snuff an' sniff around,
An' sniff an' snuff around—so's he kin find
Out where the Little Boy's hid at.—An' nen—nen—
Oh, *yes!*—W'y, purty soon the old Bear climbs
'Way out on a big limb—a grea'-long limb,—
An' nen the Little Boy climbs out the hole
An' takes his ax an' chops the limb off! . . . Nen
The old Bear falls *k-splunge!* clean to the ground
An' bust an' kill hisse'f plum' dead, he did!

An' nen the Little Boy he git his gun
An' 'menced a-climbin' down the tree ag'in—

No!—no, he *didn't* git his *gun*—'cause when
The *Bear* falled, nen the *gun* falled, too—An' broked
It all to pieces, too!—An' *nicest* gun!—
His Pa ist buyed it!—An' the Little Boy
Ist cried, he did; an' went on climbin' down
The tree—an' climbin' down—an' climbin' down!—
An'-sir! when he 'uz purt'-nigh down,—w'y, nen
The old Bear he jumped up ag'in!—an' he
Ain't dead at all—ist *'tendin'* thataway,
So he kin git the Little Boy an' eat
Him up! But the Little Boy he 'uz too smart
To climb clean *down* the tree.—An' the old Bear
He can't climb *up* the tree no more—'cause when
He fell, he broke one of his—he broke *all*
His legs!—an' nen he *couldn't* climb! But he
Ist won't go 'way an' let the Little Boy
Come down out of the tree. An' the old Bear
Ist growls 'round there, he does—ist growls an' goes
"Wooh!—Woo-ooh!" all the time! An' Little Boy
He haf to stay up in the tree—all night—
An' 'thout no *supper* neether!—On'y they
Wuz *apples* on the tree!—An' Little Boy
Et apples—ist all night—an' cried—an' cried!
Nen when 't'uz morning th' old Bear went *"Wooh!"*
Ag'in, an' try to climb up in the tree
An' git the Little Boy.—But he *can't*
Climb t'save his *soul,* he can't!—An' *oh!* he's *mad!*—
He ist tear up the ground! an' go *"Woo-ooh!"*

An'—*Oh, yes!*—purty soon, when morning's come
All *light*—so's you kin *see,* you know,—w'y, nen
The old Bear finds the Little Boy's *gun,* you know,
'At's on the ground.—(An' it ain't broke at all—
I ist *said* that!) An' so the old Bear think
He'll take the gun an' *shoot* the Little Boy:—
But *Bears they* don't know much 'bout shootin' guns:
So when he go to shoot the Little Boy,
The old Bear got the *other* end the gun
Ag'in' his shoulder, 'stid o' *th'other* end—
So when he try to shoot the Little Boy,
It shot *the Bear,* it did—an' killed him dead!
An' nen the Little Boy clumb down the tree
An' chopped his old woolly head off:—Yes, an' killed
The *other* Bear ag'in, he did—an' killed
All *boff* the bears, he did—an' tuk 'em home
An' *cooked* 'em, too, an' *et* 'em!

　　　　　　　　—An' that's all.

ON THE SUNNY SIDE

HI and whoop-hooray, boys!
    Sing a song of cheer!
    Here's a holiday, boys,
  Lasting half a year!
Round the world, and half is
  Shadow we have tried;
Now we're where the laugh is,—
  On the sunny side!

Pigeons coo and mutter,
  Strutting high aloof
Where the sunbeams flutter
  Through the stable roof.
Hear the chickens cheep, boys,
  And the hen with pride
Clucking them to sleep, boys,
  On the sunny side!

Hear the clacking guinea;
  Hear the cattle moo;
Hear the horses whinny,
  Looking out at you!

On the hitching-block, boys,
  Grandly satisfied,
See the old peacock, boys,
  On the sunny side!

Robins in the peach tree;
  Bluebirds in the pear;
Blossoms over each tree
  In the orchard there!
All the world's in joy, boys,
  Glad and glorified
As a romping boy, boys,
  On the sunny side!

Where's a heart as mellow—
  Where's a soul as free—
Where is any fellow
  We would rather be?
Just ourselves or none, boys,
  World around and wide,
Laughing in the sun, boys,
  On the sunny side!

'LIZABUTH-ANN ON BAKIN'-DAY

OUR Hired Girl, when it's bakin'-day,
　　She's out o' patience allus,
　　An' tells us "Hike *outdoors* an' play,
An' when the cookies's done," she'll say,
　"Land sake! she'll come an' call us!"
An' when the little doughbowl's all
Ist heapin'-full, she'll come an' call—
　Nen say, "She ruther take a switchin'
Than have a pack o' pesky childern
　Trackin' round the kitchen!"

183

PRIOR TO MISS BELLE'S APPEARANCE

WHAT makes you come *here* fer, Mister,
   So much to *our* house?—*Say?*
   Come to see our big sister?—
An' Charley he says 'at you kissed her
  An' he ketched you, th' uther day!—
Didn' you, Charley?—But we p'omised Belle
An' crossed our heart to never to tell—
'Cause *she* gived us some o' them-er
Chawk'lut drops 'at you bringed to her!

Charley he's my little b'uther—
   An' we has a-mostest fun,
Don't we, Charley?—Our Muther,
Whenever we whips one anuther,
   Tries to whip *us*—an' we *run*—
Don't we, Charley?—An' nen, bime-by,
Nen she gives us cake—an' pie—
Don't she, Charley?—when we come in
An' p'omise never to do it ag'in?

He's named Charley.—I'm *Willie*—
   An' I'm got the purtiest name!
But Uncle Bob *he* calls me "Billy"—
Don't he, Charley?—'N' our filly
   We named "Billy," the same
Ist like me! An' our Ma said
'At "Bob puts foolishnuss into our head!"—
Didn' she, Charley?—An' *she* don't know
Much about *boys!*—'Cause Bob said so!

Baby's a funniest feller!
   Nain't no hair on his head—
Is they, Charley?—It's meller
Wite up there! An' ef Belle er
   Us ask wuz *we* that way, Ma said,—
"Yes; an' yer *Pa's* head wuz soft as that,
An' it's that way yet!"—An' Pa grabs his hat
An' says, "Yes, childern, she's right about Pa—
'Cause that's the reason he married yer Ma!"

An' our Ma says 'at "Belle couldn'
   Ketch nothin' at all but ist *'bows'!"*—
An' *Pa* says 'at "you're soft as puddun!"—
An' *Uncle Bob* says "you're a good-un
   'Cause he can tell by yer nose!"—
Didn' he, Charley?—An' when Belle'll play
In the poller on th' pianer, some day,
Bob makes up funny songs about you,
Till she gits mad—like he wants her to!

Our sister *Fanny* she's *'leven*
  Years old! 'At's mucher 'an *I*—
'Ain't it, Charley? . . . I'm seven!—
But our sister Fanny's in *Heaven!*
  Nere's where you go ef you die!—
Don't you, Charley?—Nen you has *wings*—
Ist like Fanny!—an' *purtiest things!*—
Don't you, Charley?—An' nen you can fly—
Ist fly—an' *ever'*thing! . . . Wisht *I'd* die!

JACK THE GIANT-KILLER
BAD BOY'S VERSION

TELL you a story—an' it's a fac':—
    Wunst wuz a little boy, name wuz Jack,
    An' he had sword an' buckle an' strap
Maked of gold, an' a " 'visibul cap";
An' he killed Gi'nts 'at et whole cows—
Th' horns an' all—an' pigs an' sows!
But Jack, his golding sword wuz, oh!
So awful sharp 'at he could go
An' cut th' old Gi'nts clean in two
'Fore 'ey knowed what he wuz goin' to do!

An' *one* ole Gi'nt, he had four
Heads, an' name wuz "Bumblebore"—
An' he wuz feared o' Jack—'cause he,
Jack, he killed six—five—ten-three,
An' all o' th' uther Gi'nts but him:
An' thay wuz a place Jack haf to swim
'Fore he could git t' ole "Bumblebore"—
Nen thay wuz "griffuns" at the door:
But Jack, he thist plunged in an' swum
Clean acrost; an' when he come
To th' uther side, he thist put on
His " 'visibul cap," an' nen, dog-gone!
You couldn't see him at all!—An' so
He slewed the "griffuns"—*boff,* you know!
Nen wuz a horn hunged over his head,
High on th' wall, an' words 'at read,—
"Whoever kin this trumpet blow
Shall cause the Gi'nt's overth'ow!"
An' Jack, he thist reached up an' blowed
The stuffin' out of it! an' th'owed
Th' castul gates wide open, an'
Nen tuk his gold sword in his han',
An' thist marched in t' ole "Bumblebore,"
An', 'fore he knowed, he put 'bout four
Heads on him—an' chopped 'em off, too!—
Wisht 'at *I'd* been Jack!—don't you?

U NCLE he learns us to rhyme an' write
An' all be poets an' all recite:
His little-est poet's his little-est niece,
An' this is her little-est poetry-piece.